LESBIAN PLAYS

Jill Posener was born in London in 1953 and brought up in the Far East and in Berlin. She trained as a stage manager and worked on many shows in fringe theatre (she was the first woman in Gay Sweatshop) and in the West End. She has managed a women's rock band, The Mistakes, and since 1980 has worked as a freelance photo-journalist. Two books of her work – *Spray it Loud* and *Louder Than Words* – have been published and she is at present travelling the world researching a book on women's bodybuilding.

Libby Mason was born in 1949. She graduated from the University of Hull in 1970 with a degree in Drama and English. She has worked for seventeen years as an actress and director in alternative theatre. Among the companies with whom she has worked are The General Will, Red Ladder, The Women's Theatre Group, Gay Sweatshop and Perspectives. She is currently Director of Theatre Centre, London. She lives in London with her three-year-old daughter.

Jackie Kay was born in Edinburgh in 1961 and brought up in Glasgow. She is a poet and short-story writer as well as a playwright. Her published work includes a short story in *Stepping Out*, an anthology of short stories about female friendship, edited by Ann Oosthuizen, and poetry included in *Beautiful Barbarians*, an anthology of lesbian poetry edited by Lilian Mohin, and in *A Dangerous Knowing – Four Black Women Poets* edited by Prathiba Parmar. Since writing *Chiaroscuro* she has written a second play – *Twice Over* – which was given a rehearsed reading as part of the Gay Sweatshop Times 12 Festival in March 1987 – and written a fifteen-minute film script for BBC's *Split Screen* series. She is at present working on a collection of poetry in between doing writing workshops and teaching.

Jill Fleming was born in Forfar in 1956. She describes herself as 'a drop-out from the University of Surrey' who worked in Berlin in the late seventies and became interested in theatre in the early eighties. Her earlier plays were also performed at the Oval House Theatre, London. *The Rug of Identity* was given a second successful production in Holland in 1987 which won the Grand Prix du Théâtre.

LESBIAN PLAYS

ANY WOMAN CAN
by
Jill Posener

DOUBLE VISION
by
The Women's Theatre Group with Libby Mason

CHIAROSCURO
by
Jackie Kay

THE RUG OF IDENTITY
by
Jill W. Fleming

Selected and introduced by
Jill Davis

A Methuen Paperback

A METHUEN PAPERBACK

This volume first published in Great Britain as a Methuen paperback original in 1987 by Methuen London Ltd., 11 New Fetter Lane, London EC4P 4EE and in the United States of America by Methuen Inc., 29 West 35th Street, New York, NY 10001

British Library Cataloguing in Publication Data

Lesbian plays.—(A Methuen theatrefile).
  1. English drama—Women authors 2. English
  drama—20th century 3. Lesbianism—
  Drama
  822'.914'080353   PR1246.W65
  ISBN 0-413-15310-X

Printed in Great Britain by
Richard Clay Ltd, Bungay, Suffolk

CONTENTS

INTRODUCTION

I am writing this in March 1987, in the midst of an increasing public debate, sparked off by the AIDS epidemic, around the family, morality, sexuality and, particularly, homosexuality. Hearing the strong popular antipathy to homosexuality which is being articulated, it would seem difficult to hold to the argument (the argument, indeed, which underpins the 'brother' series to this, *Gay Plays*) that homosexuality is merely a matter of private choice and nothing to do with 'politics'.

If, by politics we mean not just party politics (although clearly the political parties have an increasing interest in the issue), but all those matters which touch on a person's rights as a citizen, then clearly homosexuality does have political implications. Knowledge of a person's sexual orientation can materially affect employment, career advancement, access to housing and welfare benefits. Male homosexuality is circumscribed by the law, and the fear of AIDS may now jeopardise a gay man's rights to medical treatment. These are all matters which affect economic, social and even physical survival. They are political matters.

It seems to me that those who want to claim that sexual preference is a minor matter are able to do so because they, as individuals, are able to mitigate the effects of discrimination by other forms of power, eg, the power of being middle-class and white and because in the past twenty years homosexual people have enjoyed as great a liberty as has ever been permitted them in this country. But to ignore the fact that this liberty was won by political activity is to close one's eyes to the fact that that 'permission' could be withdrawn at any time as a result of political activity from another quarter.

At present the Member of Parliament who advocated on my television screen last night the criminalisation of all homosexual activity (including, for the first time, that of lesbians) is out on a political limb. But his views are popular, in the truest sense.

The position from which I decided to put together a volume of lesbian plays is one which does claim that homosexuality is a political matter. It proposes that human sexuality is shaped by, and can be understood by reference to, the specific political and ideological system within which an individual is brought up. This is a view which rejects a purely biological, or purely psychological, explanation of sexuality. It is what is meant by 'sexual politics', which is the political project of both the Gay and Women's movements.

It is a crucial method of explanation for homosexual people since it allows us to understand not just homosexuality, but also why it is so feared and hated in our society. This hatred, often referred to as homophobia, is not simply to be found in heterosexual people but often lies deep in the homosexual person's view of her/himself. In this sense homosexual people may be seen as a disadvantaged group experiencing, in common with other oppressed groups, both explicit forms of discrimination from the majority group and an internalised sense of 'deserving it', of inferiority or deviancy. The latter is the reason why the former is not resisted.

The first phase of liberation for any such group is the recognition of the forms of oppression, internal and external, and the attempt to combat these by promoting new images of and for the group. In this theoretical writing is central (and I commend the work of Jeffrey Weeks to anyone who is interested in the politics of homosexuality), but in the demonstration of ideas to a wider audience, art is also a 'political weapon'. The theatre, particularly, has a long history of being just that.

European theatre has its roots in propaganda, albeit for the status quo, and British theatre became, early in its history, a public platform for competing political views. It is for this reason that it was subject to strict legal control for so long.

In the twentieth century the theatre has been used as a campaign tool by the Suffrage Movement (some of which plays are published by Methuen) and by the Communist Workers' Theatre Movement of the 1920s and 30s. The growth of alternative theatre in the 1970s will be familiar territory to many of the readers of this book. Such theatre companies as The General Will, Belt and Braces, Broadside Mobile, CAST, and a host of other companies – including 7:84 (Scotland) and Red Ladder who continue that work – reintroduced the idea of a theatre which opposes the status quo. None of these companies was affiliated to a particular party, but all shared a socialist commitment to creating theatre for and about working-class people which promoted a socialist critique of society.

That so many of these companies are no longer in existence should not be interpreted as an end to oppositional theatre. The truth is that that energy, in theatre as in the socialist movement, has gone into new channels and new forms. Influenced very particularly by the politics of the feminist, Black and Gay movements, the Left's idea of the 'underclass' has broadened from a single focus on the working-class to a complex focus on the diversity of groups who are disadvantaged and excluded from power. Amongst these would be women, Blacks and Asians, members of other ethnic minorities, gays and lesbians, the aged and disabled.

As the Labour local authorities of the 1980s may be seen to be putting into practice policies which positively discriminate in favour of such groups and in so doing recognising the diversity of communities in their geographical area, so political theatre in the 1980s has redefined itself as community theatre.

The community a theatre company serves may be geographically defined: there are theatre companies in Britain serving particular areas, usually those which are geographically isolated, or whose community interests are not served by other forms of theatre, for example, an inner city housing estate, a mining community. A community may also be defined on a non-geographical basis, that is, by a community of interest. There are theatre companies working in Britain serving all of the disadvantaged groups I referred to earlier, and others.

All four of the plays in this anthology were produced by theatre companies who exist to serve a defined community. Gay Sweatshop is Britain's oldest gay theatre company, and *Any Woman Can* was its first lesbian play; The Women's Theatre Group, who produced *Double Vision*, was Britain's first feminist theatre company; Hard Corps, who produced *The Rug of Identity* is a lesbian theatre company, and Theatre of Black Women exists to serve the community of Black women in this country with work that explores racism, sexism and, in *Chiaroscuro*, heterosexism. In all of these companies those people who produce the work are never simply hired labour but always part of the community whose interests they exist to promote.

I hope the publication of the four plays produced by these companies will introduce readers who have not seen them to their work, and to the work of the four writers. Not only, I hope, through reading but by encouraging people to go and see the companies, and to consider further productions of these plays. Writers, directors, actors and all the others who create this kind of theatre, work in conditions of hardship. Reward, both in terms of subsidy to pay a living wage, and in the form of public recognition of the work, is scant.

I also hope that the publication of the first British anthology of lesbian plays will encourage more new writing by/for lesbians. The number of plays in print which represent lesbians is very small: Sarah Daniel's plays *Neaptide* and *The Devil's Gateway* (published by Methuen), Gay Sweatshop and Michelene Wandor's *Care and Control*, Michelene Wandor's *AID Thy Neighbour*, Alison Lyssa's *Pinball*, Maro Green and Caroline Griffin's *More* (both published in Methuen's *Plays by Women* series) and *Basin* by Jacqueline Rudet (published in Methuen's *Black Plays*) are the only ones I know of.

This perhaps begins to answer an unacknowledged question, why lesbian plays? By comparison with the number of plays by gay men accessible in print and in Britain's larger theatres, lesbian theatre might be thought not to exist. In 1986/87 there were four plays about gay men in West End theatres – *Torch Song Trilogy* and *La Cage Aux Folles* by Harvey Fierstein, *The Normal Heart* by Larry Kramer and *Breaking the Code* by Hugh Whitemore.

It is ironic that although when the popular voice most clearly expresses its antipathy to homosexuality it is nearly always referring to male homosexuality, plays, films, and television dramas about homosexuals far more commonly feature gay men than lesbians. Two of Britain's most popular soap operas, *East Enders* and *Brookside* have central characters who are gay men, but lesbians are almost invisible. *Brookside* did briefly introduce a minor character who was lesbian but clearly lesbians are not allowed to live on the close or in the square . . .

Part of my motivation to edit this anthology was a desire to correct this imbalance of representation and to make visible the fact that lesbians do exist, do write plays and that there is a lesbian theatre. Also to correct another form of imbalance: a visit to any women's bookshop will reveal a growing amount of writing by lesbians, in the form of novels, poetry, short stories and theoretical writing. Plays, of course, belong first and last in performance, but when plays are not published they disappear from history and little is left to a future generation of theatre historians and practitioners. In editing this volume I would like very much to have included a play by, about, for lesbian women written before 1945. I haven't found one. I am not surprised, since theatre is the most public of all art forms and I doubt that such a play would have received a licence for performance. Having failed to receive a performance its chances of an after-life, through publication, are small. (If, however, readers do know of such a script I would be delighted to learn of it.)

I have so far answered the question 'why lesbian plays?' by comparing the invisibility of lesbian theatre with the higher theatrical visibility of gay men. This is not a complete justification for this anthology since one might legitimately ask whether lesbians are not, ought not to be, represented within feminist theatre writing. The answer is, rarely. As I have already indicated, only two plays in our 'sister' series *Plays By Women* are on lesbian subjects. This is not intended as a criticism of the editors of that series; their choice accurately represents the extent of inclusion of lesbians within the mainstream of women's theatre writing.

Explanation of this, and therefore a full justification of a separate space for lesbian theatre writing, lies in the history of the sexual politics movements of the past two decades.

Those lesbian women who began to define their sexuality as a political issue did so at first as part of the Gay Liberation movement of the early 1970s. Many became disenchanted, feeling that movement to be dominated by issues affecting gay men which did not affect gay women, for example, the law and male sexual practice rather than the law and lesbian mothers. At the same time the early Women's movement's analyses of sexism allowed lesbians to see male-centredness in the Gay movement as a replication of male-centredness in the society as a whole. Many lesbians came to see themselves as having interests in common with other women rather than with gay men. (That development can be seen paralleled by developments within Gay Sweatshop. In 1977 the company split into two autonomous groups, one male, one female, a move promoted by the women of the company. The women's first show after the split was *Care and Control*, a play about the law's definition of a 'fit' mother.)

The theoretical explorations and political campaigns of the Women's movement of the late 1970s can be seen reflected in some of the theatre which developed around it. Two plays by feminist writers, *AID They Neighbour* by Michelene Wandor (1978) and *Cloud Nine* by Caryl Churchill (1979), have patterns of action and final images which seem to me to signify what the Women's movement saw as the political project of the late seventies.

In *AID Thy Neighbour* two couples are trying to conceive children. One couple is lesbian, the other heterosexual. The play is a comedy which has as its hilarious centrepiece the (thwarted) attempt by a woman journalist to write a gutter press 'scandal' about lesbian mothers and artificial insemination. It ends with Georgina, who is lesbian, having become pregnant, and Mary, who is heterosexual, having realised that she does not want a child. Together with their partners, (Sandy, a lesbian who has reservations about parenthood) and Joe (a man who passionately wants a child), they decide to pull down the dividing wall between their homes and live communally with their friend Daphne and her child.

This offering of new definitions of the family, questioning of gender-roles, and emphasis on homosexuality as a key part of those redefinitions is found again in *Cloud Nine*. Having shown, in a first Act set in Colonial Africa, the links between capitalism, imperialism and the oppression of women and homosexuals, the second Act shows the characters defining their own 'cloud nine' – a way of living which liberates rather than oppresses. Here the 'new family' consists of Vic, her lesbian lover, Lin, Vic's brother, Eddy, and the two women's children. Eddy's male lover is on the periphery of this family, and Vic's mother, having divorced her patriarchal husband, seems set to join it. Significantly, the only character who is excluded from it, by his own inability to engage with the politics of sexuality, is the one heterosexual man, Vic's husband.

Those, however, were the images and dreams of the 70s. Things are different in the late 1980s. In Britain we have seen both a rightward shift of social policy under a Conservative government and Labour administrations in some of the cities putting positive discrimination policies into practice. Perhaps it is defensiveness in reaction to the first or the realities of administration of the second that have led to a discernible shift of political emphasis in the liberal and socialist parts of the Women's movement.

Whatever the causes, there are clear signs that those feminists are now centering their debates and campaigns around the nuclear, rather than the 'new' family, on ways of co-operating with men rather than challenging men and their sexism, and on domestic labour rather than public attitudes to women's sexuality. Although some of these issues are relevant to lesbians as women, the central issue that concerns them – the profound ambivalence to women's sexuality which marks this society, and of which lesbians are particular victims – seems to have been put 'on the back burner' of the Women's movement of the 1980s.

Lesbian women, then, often feel that neither the Women's movement, in its 'pro-family' phase, nor the Gay movement, which is inevitably preoccupied by campaigns around AIDS (a disease which exclusively lesbian women are very unlikely to contract – so much for God's wrath . . .) is appropriately representing their interests. This feeling is voiced in the editorial collective's introduction to the first issue of *Gossip* in 1986: 'Many of us have felt silenced in the last few years as the Women's Liberation movement drifts further and further away from feminism and lesbianism towards humanism, socialism and liberalism.'

Gossip is a journal issuing from lesbian radical feminism, and this represents an observable tendency in the late 1980s, that is, the fragmentation of the Women's movement into a plurality of feminisms. As the Women's movement in its origins claimed a separate space for women, so that claim is being repeated within the movement by groups of women who feel that their particularity is unrepresented. Lesbian feminists form one such group, but Black feminists and working-class feminists too have formed their own groupings, away from what has been seen as a mainstream feminism over-dominated by white, middle-class, heterosexual women.

Some of these developments are already visible in women's theatre in the 1980s. Caryl Churchill is a socialist feminist playwright whose 70s plays *Vinegar Tom*, *Light Shining in Buckinghamshire* and *Cloud Nine* all focused on sexual relations as the key to women's oppression. Interestingly, her 1980s plays have focused on women in the public world (in *Top Girls*, which implicitly criticises liberal feminism's demand for more women in positions of power), on working-class women (in *Fen*) and, in *A Mouthful of Birds*, the play she co-wrote with David Lan in 1986, on an explicit rejection of the association made by radical feminism of violence and 'maleness'.

Liberal feminist playwrights, whose work unsurprisingly constitutes the majority of plays by women performed on main stages, seem most often to be preoccupied by the issue of balancing women's demand for space in the public world of work, with their personal destiny as mothers and (heterosexual) lovers. Many such playwrights are heard to be irritated when asked questions about their politics, demanding the same right as male playwrights to write as individuals, rather than as spokeswomen for feminism. That position is totally understandable, but the consequence is that much of the most visible women's theatre writing in the 1980s leaves feminists and lesbians disheartened by its lack of political energy.

So far, few of the plays which come from radical/lesbian feminism have made their way into print or onto the larger stages, although in the 'Women's circuit' of venues in the major cities such work is a clearly visible phenomenon of the eighties. Sarah Daniels is one such playwright whose work is in print and her work has been performed at the Royal Court Theatre and at the Cottesloe, the smallest of the National Theatre's stages. Her plays tackle the major issues of the radical feminist agenda, for example, pornography and rape in *Masterpieces*, lesbianism and heterosexism in *Neaptide*.

Black women's theatre is also a phenomenon of the 80s. Existing Black and Asian theatre companies have begun to present work by women, and in 1982 Britain's, indeed Europe's, first Black women's theatre company, Theatre of Black Women, was formed. Again, this is a theatrical development with a strong audience demand which so far has remained relatively invisible on the main stages and in print, although Jacqueline Rudet's work has been presented at the Royal Court and two of her plays are in print – *Money to Live* is in *Plays By Women, Vol. 5*, and *Basin* in *Black Plays*.

I hope by now that I have made a case for the publication of a volume of specifically lesbian plays – it parallels the development of lesbian politics, lesbian communities and a lesbian culture. That said, however, my selection of plays for this anthology has been made to reflect a diversity of perspectives on lesbian issues, not to represent a particular political or cultural view. Of the playwrights whose work is represented here, one is black, three are white; two are Scottish, two English; two are in their twenties, two in their thirties. If this volume initiates a series I would like to widen this range, especially to include plays by older, and younger, women about issues which concern lesbians in those age groups, and to include plays about the experience of lesbians in other ethnic groups.

Theatrically, what these plays have in common is that all were produced within the poverty of small, underfunded theatre companies which limits the writer's choices of cast size and theatrical effects. Three were presented on national tours as well as in London venues and portability again imposes limits upon a writer's freedom. Each of the plays, however, makes a different response to these limits. Jill Posener's play *Any*

Woman Can uses the simplest of theatrical forms, a series of intercut monologues and short dialogues to express, as she says in her afterword, 'those things that were most dear to me'. *Double Vision* is a devised play which reflects the input of all the members of the group who produced it and uses Brechtian techniques of songs and narration to comment on the action as well as a series of three alternative endings. Jackie Kay is principally a poet and her play *Chiaroscuro* reflects that in its structure and in the use of poetry and song as expressive devices. *The Rug of Identity*, by Jill Fleming, is a farce, using the conventions of that genre – confused identities, unknown parentages etc – in a manner reminiscent of Joe Orton's plays.

Each of the plays explores lesbian identity from a different perspective. *Any Woman Can* explores the pain of 'coming out', recognising and declaring oneself as a lesbian. It was written in 1975 and I include it both because it is a piece of history – it was the first lesbian play presented by Gay Sweatshop – and because I suspect that the fears and miseries of the central character are still being experienced by lesbians, especially those out of reach of the lesbian communities of the big cities. *Chiaroscuro*, written in 1986, also explores coming out, but in a different context. Here awareness of racial identity is as crucial as awareness of lesbian identity, and the group of black women who are the central characters are seen to become stronger and closer as their understanding of racism and sexism grows. *Double Vision* (1982) is also a play in which being lesbian is not seen as a separate or single issue. The play shows, through a series of domestic scenes, the ways in which class difference and political difference define a 'private' relationship. As Libby Mason writes in her afterword, it is a play intended to 'have resonance for heterosexual and gay women and men who experience the area of "relationships" as a significant political battlefield.' The final play in the anthology, *The Rug of Identity*, is not a campaigning, or explaining, or exploring play, but a comedy of manners, the manners of a metropolitan lesbian community. In that, it takes for granted an audience of lesbians secure enough in their identity to watch 'The Rug' being pulled from under it and from under the shibboleths of feminist politics, and to find it very funny. That seems to me to be a mark of the self-confidence of lesbians to which I would like the publication of this anthology to be a contribution.

Jill Davis
1987

ANY WOMAN CAN

Any Woman Can was first performed at the Haymarket Studio Theatre, Leicester, in November 1975. It was given further performances by Gay Sweatshop during its lunchtime season at the ICA Theatre, London, which opened in February 1976, after which the play toured nationally and to Dublin.

The play was performed with a cast of four or five and the following is a list of the actresses who performed the play at various points in its Gay Sweatshop production.

Brenda Addie
Helen Barnaby
Donna Champion
Kate Crutchley
Nancy Diuguid
Patricia Donovan
Vanessa Forsyth

Sandra Freeman
Patricia Garwood
Sara Hardy
Elizabeth Lindsay
Penelope Nice
Julie Parker

Director: Kate Crutchley
Designer: Mary Moore

Characters

GINNY
HEADMISTRESS
ANN
JEAN
MRS ALLAN
JULIE
VOICE
OLDER WOMAN
DEBBIE
THREE WOMEN

GINNY *enters and speaks to the audience. The other members of the cast are sitting amongst the audience.*

GINNY: You are looking at a screaming
   lesbian.
A raving dyke,
A pervert, deviant,
Queer, fairy, fruitcake, freak,
Daughter, sister, niece, mother, cousin,
Mother-in-law,
Clippie, actress, bishop's wife, MP,
Machinist, typist, teacher, char,
I'm everywhere.
In your armies, in your schools,
peering at you out of passing trains,
sitting down next to you on the
   crowded bus
in seat D22, yes sir, right next to you.
I'm here to stay
to infiltrate
to convert.
Mary, Mary if you're there, are you
   aware
that at your festival of Blight, in your
   congregation of 20,000
19,000 of your little lambs were
   standing next to perverts
just like me?
Harrowing thought, isn't it?
Just think, at this precise moment there
   are lesbian nurses touching up lovely
   women in hospitals, quite legally . . .
adjusting their dressings round their
   injured thighs,
washing, rubbing, massaging . . . oh
   stop it . . .
Oh yes, we're meant to be the perverts,
but let me tell you that hardly a week
goes by without my getting a phone call
from one of the world's great wankers,
asking if he can come and suck me off
and telling me I won't be gay if I sleep
with him. And then there was the
heavy breather at 5 a.m. on Christmas
morning. Talk about good will to all
men. And the funny thing is that they
are all young men with middle-class
accents, and they are all sick. It's not a
'giant step' from sexual assault on the
phone to sexual assault on your
daughter. You may be wondering how
they all have my phone number. No,
actually, I didn't have 10,000 tiny
stickers run off at enormous expense to
stick in car windows, public loos and
tube stations. Put a flatshare ad in
Time Out and see for yourself. Being a
lesbian isn't all bad though. We do
have our laughs occasionally.
   I'd like to tell you about me. Me,
jolly Ginny, compassionate Ginny, who
used to fight to help a fellow gay find
the strength to 'come out' but who went
home alone. Ginny who spent her days
in the company of others, laughing,
joking, camping it up. I was the loudest
mouth, and the loneliest.

HEADMISTRESS *enters from audience.*

HEADMISTRESS: Welcome. Wipe your
feet on my Timothy Whites bristle mat,
stroke my dogs, my fawning cocker
spaniels, spread your little bum on my
loose covers, warm your thighs by my
open fire, touch my knee. This once.
Look at my bookshelves, admire my
priceless vases, sip my tea, eat my
gingernuts. Take advantage of it. This
is your first day at our boarding school
nestled in the Titsey Hills and we love
you. Then do the slow-foot shuffle
through the red-tiled corridors, up the
wooden staircase to the sparse cold
dormitory. From here on in we'll
punish you for being here, we'll do our
best to reform you and those who won't
conform to our little kingdom's rules,
we'll simply do away with. We shall
reject, deject, degrade, dehumanise, de
this, de that. There'll be a convenient
bottle of pills, a razor blade, or a
kitchen knife in the common room
because we know you'll never do it.
You are ours, your mind and being,
your tits and lips, there for the taking, a
whipping girl for me and a scapegoat
for 200 little brats to whose parents I
am ever grateful.

GINNY: Sometimes they make me an
apple-pie bed with a difference. When I
pull back the covers I find they have
smeared tomato ketchup all over the
sheets. They all know who did it but
they say, 'Look, Ginny is dirty,
Ginny's bleeding all over her bed.'
Sometimes I think I'll never get out of
here. Some weekends when my mother
isn't able to come and take me out.
Sometimes when I sob into my pillow
and there's the pain of stifling my tears.
When the teasing and mockery become
unbearable and I hit out wildly in self-
defence, only to be locked up for my
viciousness. The teachers don't have to

punish girls who are cruelly and ceaselessly tormented by others. There's a wood just beyond this window pane. If I could prise open the window I could touch the leaves, but the window is nailed shut and there are bars across the frame. I often wonder whether it is to keep us from falling out, as they say, or whether they know there are some of us willing to jump in order to escape. Well, instead here are thoughts of slashed wrists and rusty razor blades sliding through thirteen-year-old skin. Sometimes I feel I'll never get out of here, as I rock to sleep, clutching my pillow to my body, grasping, holding, loving.

HEADMISTRESS *stands.*

HEADMISTRESS: Masturbating again, Virginia?

GINNY: I'm back in the room I know so well, visits are becoming so frequent I might as well move in! She stares at me and waits for an answer. She actually expects me to answer 'yes' or 'no', and if I say 'no' the best I can expect is a sharp rap across the face.

HEADMISTRESS: Were you masturbating in class again, Virginia? Well? I can see I shall have to fetch Miss Blackmore. Wait.

HEADMISTRESS *exits to audience.*

GINNY: Yes, you bitch I was. Yes, yes, yes. Sometimes I think I'll die in here. When the lights go out I think I am dead, only to be roused at seven, wash hastily, dress, sit silent for five long gruelling minutes and run like well-oiled machines to the common and back, ticked off a list by the ubiquitous prefects. Sometimes I think I'll die in here when my head is sick and there's not a letter in days.

I slashed my wrists today as I sat in the regulation six inches of bath water. I checked the temperature and eased the blade across my arm. I felt the blood today as the trickle became a stream, as the blood flowed. I didn't die in there. My half hour was up and there was banging on the door and shouting. I didn't lock the door because not even that place could make me want to die that much. As they put me to bed someone touched my face, the first sign

of love in two long years. We agreed to meet in her room. We'd planned it weeks in advance – but even then I suppose neither of us knew if we'd really go through with it. I watched her come in, her legs were the first things I saw as I sat on the bed, my eyes glued to the floor not daring to look up and see her face. The legs stopped. I could tell what she was thinking just by watching those legs. I knew that she was so happy to see me. I didn't look at her face, so she knelt down. Her face glowed, I mean really glowed. I don't remember what she said to me, something trite like 'Hello, nice to see you.' I just remember that my heart was throbbing. I couldn't breathe and my body was shaking even before I felt her warm hand on my shoulder. It occurred to me then what we were doing. This was the secret lesbian affair in a girls' boarding school that one never reads about in the staple diet of girls comics or in *Jill's Adventures at St Jude's*. She smiled but I was growing more and more frightened by the minute. I'd be the one to get expelled, my only distinction in life was being the most punished girl in 4B. She sat on the bed, it made the most awful creaking noise, we couldn't help laughing. There was nothing to be said, she just very gently undressed me, touched me so sweetly and took off her clothes. We just clung to each other. There was so much pain released. I ached. I remember every moment of that night. I can feel every single touch of her hands, her lips, her body, every moment. I'd been there for two years, she for seven. This was the night we had both been longing for. For – well for what? – for the release of all our hatred, all our misery at that place. For a few days I was euphoric, nothing seemed to bother me. Not the morning runs, nor the inane grin of the preacher, learning Archimedes Principle in that pokey physics building in the woods, the assemblies, those awful meals, queuing in silence. May the Lord make us truly . . .

ANN *enters reading a letter.*

ANN: Ginny, as you know, I take 'A' levels soon.

GINNY: Within a month she wasn't even smiling at me.

ANN: Perhaps it would be better if you didn't come to my room anymore. I really ought to try thinking a bit more seriously about my future. And of course I've got a lot of swotting to do. I'd love to keep seeing you of course but I think it best if we just forget what happened. Ann. Please destroy this.

GINNY: I was shattered. I had imagined we were the only two of our kind and she was opting out. I wandered around, my face swollen, with tears bursting out of me.

JEAN *enters from audience reading a letter.*

JEAN: Dear Ginny, I miss you. I wish you were back. London's very lonely without you. What have you been doing with yourself? Dave and I went to Windsor Great Park yesterday. It was so funny. We parked the car and started to walk towards what we thought was the zoo, but about one and a half hours later we ran into an electric fence and realised we'd gone slightly wrong. Well we spent the next hour trying to find the path we'd been on originally but we kept going round in circles. By this time it was getting dark so we decided to shout in the hope that someone might hear. The prospect of spending a night in the park in the middle of November didn't really appeal to either of us. Luckily a warden in his Landrover heard us and came tearing through the trees. He'd noticed our car on one of his earlier rounds and took us straight back. It was about midnight when we got home. It was really funny.

GINNY: Like constipation.

JEAN *continues to read letter.*

JEAN: I know that Dave and I can never be more than friends. Don't ask me how I know, I just do. He's a very sweet man and I like him as a friend, but I love you. I'll meet you at the station on Tuesday. My love, Jean.

GINNY: She did meet me at the station. It was terrible. I don't like to think of our relationship in its death throes. Very ugly. She married the man she couldn't be more than friends with. I saw her recently, she looked me up!

She said she felt no more guilt and wanted us to become friends again. She said I had been the best friend she ever had. No, she couldn't tell Dave she was seeing me again. His attitude hadn't changed in five years – he wouldn't understand.

JEAN: He's a very kind person.

GINNY: Oh I am pleased.

JEAN: I hope you don't mind me looking you up after all this time. I felt a need to . . . I wanted to see you, ask if you are happy.

GINNY: Yes I am and I don't mind at all. Is that all you wanted to know, whether I'm happy?

JEAN: What else would there be?

GINNY: Maybe you wanted to see whether you still reacted to me the way you used to. To test your heterosexuality.

JEAN: Maybe. I'm confused about what happened to us, Ginny. It doesn't fit in with my life as I know it now. I want us to be friends again.

GINNY: Friends? Jean, we were lovers. I remember when you first met Dave. He used to say how great it was that you had a girlfriend you really cared about. And then you told him. You told him everything about us.

JEAN: I had to tell him the truth.

GINNY: After that, he stopped me seeing you. Everywhere you went he was always there. Like the time I went to meet you at the swimming baths and he came out first. I pleaded with him. I just want to be her friend. I don't want to lose her entirely.

JEAN: You threatened everything he believed in, he couldn't understand.

GINNY: He said he never wanted me to see you again. He said you wanted the same.

JEAN: I was going to marry him. I wish we could be close again.

GINNY: But you can't tell him you're seeing me again. From one guilt to another. You're still ashamed of what we did, you're ashamed of treating me the way you did. You're ashamed of yourself. You wish it had never happened and messed up your cosy respectability. But it did and you should be happy that it did. Don't be ashamed. Will I see you again?

JEAN: Yes, it would be nice.

GINNY: I'll phone you.

JEAN: Yes, but don't phone in the evenings.

JEAN *exits to audience.*

GINNY: My greatest fear was that I was the only *one*. I knew in my mind somewhere that there must be another one, but would I meet her in Clapham? Could I be sure that she would live in the same town as me, and how would I recognise her? And she me? The fear of loneliness, the same fear and the same pain I'd felt at school brought home to me the awful fact that 'she', whoever I thought she was, was not going to accost me in the last row of the cinema and whisper the magic words 'I'm a lesbian too' in my ear.

GINNY *crosses to* MRS ALLAN *sitting in audience.*

GINNY: Can I talk to you, Mrs Allan? I mean ... um ... I feel I can talk to you.

MRS ALLAN: Of course, love, come and sit down.

GINNY: I think I prefer women to men. Oh but only as friends, of course. (Christ what am I saying?) I think I'm a lesbian.

MRS ALLAN: Well what are you worried about? Everybody's doing it these days. Be a bit promiscuous for a while.

GINNY: You don't understand. I've not admitted it to myself yet. It's easy for you heterosexuals. You're encouraged to show your sexual colours as soon as you can crawl. Sex for me becomes an immense problem to be concealed or at best explained away as a passing phase.

MRS ALLAN: I've never slept with a woman. I've never even wanted to before. Well, it was so long ago it hardly counts, but there was this woman, a chauffeuse, who I met at John's hotel when she was collecting her boss. He was a washing-machine manufacturer, and I was looking through their advertising pamphlets when this woman appeared. We spent the rest of the afternoon discussing the merits of top-loading machines, but I felt a physical excitement just being close to that woman, something which I've never felt with anyone else. Would you like to stay here tonight? Or phone me sometimes? John is never here on Tuesdays or Wednesdays. I find you very attractive, so stay.

GINNY: I was stunned! Was that what it was like? This wasn't 'coming out' as I had imagined it, proud and confident, 'Liberation'. This was furtive, very un-proud, a quick lay on Tuesdays, maybe Wednesdays, at her choosing, in the depths of Penge. Plain, simple sexual gratification, though in retrospect there wasn't much of that either. She was so nastily clinical about it ...

MRS ALLAN: I didn't think you'd come here to watch television.

MRS ALLAN *exits to seat in audience.*

GINNY: Sex didn't seem to be what I wanted. I needed to know that women could love each other because they had chosen to do so, not as a furtive fuck when hubby was out of town. I read an article in a women's magazine with the cheerful heading 'It's not all gaiety' and I felt I needed to get in touch with women who were happy to be lesbians. It takes a lot of time when you're surrounded by the 'norm' to realise that the 'norm' is not necessarily right for you. After years of confusion I finally made my first phone call to a gay organisation, CHE, the Campaign for Homosexual Equality. A man answered. I hung up. I rang again and he suggested I call by on a particular night and see the woman on duty. But it seemed to me then that walking through that door was tantamount to making my sexuality public property. To me it meant once I'd done it there was no going back, I couldn't change my mind. (I tend to see things in very uncompromising terms, in extremes.) When I eventually rang the bell of the office I was panic-stricken. What if it's all a front for some ghastly police trap and they frame me for some obscure crime like loitering with intent? What will I say to my first real-life in-the-flesh-declared lesbian? She terrified me.

I thought, 'My God it's a man.' She wasn't, she'd just had a haircut and the hairdresser had gone a bit beserk. She was one of the kindest people I'd ever met and after chatting for a while she said very matter of factly, 'You mustn't think of falling for me' – as most newcomers did. Latch on to the first lesbian that comes along, because you never know, close your eyes for a moment and she might disappear and there might never be another one. I know I felt like that. She asked me whether I'd like to go to a gay club for a drink with her and her girlfriend. More of them! There's more of them! Us, I mean. It was so overwhelming. At first I said 'no'. I felt I might be overcome by the sight of more women. Suddenly through one little door and I was there. Home and dry, I thought.

The gay scene can be the coldest and loneliest place in the world, tightly packed as it is into clubs and pubs, too tight to say hello. There we all are – tightly closeted together. From our individual cubby-holes into one enormous suite. The feelings the same, only now I could see the feeling on a thousand other faces as well. For me, that was progress.

GINNY *and* JULIE *dance, chat, kiss, then break. Light change.*

GINNY: Explain to me.

JULIE: You know why. I'm not a lesbian, you know I'm not, it's unfair to you to make demands.

GINNY: You love me, don't you? You've just said you love me.

JULIE: Yes I love you, but I can't touch you. I do love you but I can't.

GINNY: Are you ever going to be able to?

JULIE: I'm not sure. Perhaps not. I don't know.

GINNY: Do you see our touching each other as just sex? What stops you wanting me physically? Is it guilt? Fear? We are lovers. We live together, we kiss, we hold hands, we sleep in the same bed, we acknowledge our love for one another and you say you're not a lesbian. We don't fuck, that's all. That's not the only thing that matters,

can't you see that? So what is it you're afraid of? If my body turns you off, why do you sleep with me, kiss my lips, stroke my hair?

JULIE: It's not you, you know that, it's very unfair of you to turn it into me not fancying you, very unfair and cruel. We've been through all this before. It's sex that makes it so definite. I don't know that I'm ready yet. Don't push me, please.

GINNY: I want to touch you, Julie, because I love you.

JULIE: Why don't you sleep with other people?

GINNY: Because I believe in monogamy, I suppose. I don't know.

JULIE: But we're not making love so it's not a question of being faithful to one lover.

GINNY: That's hardly the point, is it? Anyhow wouldn't you be jealous?

JULIE: Would that matter?

GINNY: Of course.

JULIE: Why should it?

GINNY: I don't want to hurt you, I don't want to sleep with anyone else. I only want you.

JULIE: But there's no chance for us, not really. If you were a man everything would be all right, I can see I'll go back to men.

GINNY: You couldn't, not now.

JULIE: It wouldn't be the same, but it's the only way I seem to know.

GINNY: But that wasn't what you wanted.

JULIE: At least it's familiar. After all this time I can't let you touch me. With men it's a totally instinctive thing. Call me a coward if you like. Say it's a cop-out. I can't change.

GINNY: You're talking about sex. What we have is so much more than that. Us, together, women loving each other, helping, comforting, consoling, everything. What you're talking about is a Saturday night fuck, habitual sex. You hate it, but it's what you're used to. Christ.

JULIE: What do you want me to do? This

is no good for you or any other woman I get involved with. I can't go through life explaining – I'm sorry but I can't make love. I'm a lesbian but I can't have sex with another woman. Thanks. I'd rather not have to explain.

GINNY: Julie, let's talk about it . . .

JULIE: Can we stop talking about it now? I'm tired. I don't want to think about it. I do know I love you and I know I want to be with you but I just can't . . .

JULIE *exits to seat in audience.*

GINNY: So she left. She really did. I understood, I suppose; well, no, I didn't. I couldn't comprehend how anyone could go back to a man after experiencing love with a woman. I often wonder what happened to her. I thought it best not to keep in touch. Last time I heard from her she was seeing this lecturer. Quite a nice man really, in fact I'd always thought he was homosexual himself. Perhaps he is . . .? Maybe he's done the same thing to his male lover. Julie had never been happy with men, which is why she wandered down to the club where we met. She loved me but she was determined not to touch or be touched by another woman. She never totally committed herself and that was her escape back to the straight world. She didn't hurt me, she was too loving to hurt me, but I don't like to think what she's done to herself.

JULIE *leaves. One of the characters sitting in the audience speaks to* GINNY.

VOICE: Try the Gateways.

GINNY: I've never been there before. I don't know that I'd dare to go alone.

VOICE: You might even get frisked at the door.

GINNY: Not with my luck.
Knock thrice . . . peephole opens.
Not a member? Sorry, members only.
Well, can I become a member?
No you can't.
Why not?
You have to come with a member.
But I don't know any.
Tough.
Slam.
So I wandered down to the Coleherne and the Boltons and found there were

no women, rang the bell of some long-defunct group in Notting Hill and footed it back to the Gates where they'd turned me down ten times before. Would you take me in please? I don't know anyone, you see. (*Pause.*) Down the ol' meat market with all the gays on display, the shop window of the gay scene. In clubs and up the pubs, leaning against hoardings, corner of alley secret places, palm trees dressing the dimly lit, lino-floored ghetto bars. Jukeboxes loud and grotesquely wailing. Overcharging, private club style for membership of this select élite of social outcasts. By Appointment to the Queen on the wall, along with postcards of Morecambe and East Sussex resorts in the sunshine. Are you being served? Is anyone being served?

OLDER WOMAN *enters from audience but does not direct this speech to* GINNY.

OLDER WOMAN: Where's my dinner? I said I'd be back at seven. I'm supposed to be at the club in twenty minutes. Did you iron my shirt? The blue one. You know I always wear the blue one when I play darts. Did you get the stain off my tie? Are you going to your mother's tonight? I'm not sure when I'll be home. I'll phone. Did you get the family allowance for the kids? In your purse? I'll just take three. You seen my lighter? I thought I had it when we were over at Jo and Barbara's. I haven't seen it since then. You what? Where? Oh yes, so it is. Did you buy me some beer? I might bring Jo back with me. Well if you haven't, could you pop to the corner and fetch some in? Look, forget dinner, I've got to be going, I'll eat later. When you hear the phone, don't answer. I'll let it ring twice and then hang up. Give you time to put the dinner on. See you.

OLDER WOMAN *crosses to the 'club' area.*

GINNY: The air is close, closets are usually stale, the lighting theatrically tasteless – we see each other, glamorised in the reddish gleam. Tinted flesh in the half light. Dancing couples, foursomes drinking in corners, some chatting up at the bar, some 'deft' rebuffs. Haven't I seen all this somewhere before, down the ol' meat market of the straight scene.

Music is playing. The OLDER WOMAN *appears beside* GINNY. *Their talk is not heard over the music. The music stops.*

OLDER WOMAN: Your place?

They leave the 'club' area.

OLDER WOMAN: Not a palace, is it?

GINNY: It's my home.

OLDER WOMAN: Come on then, let's get to bed. Why are you shaking? Nervous? No need to be nervous. You'll like it. Haven't you ever been picked up in a bar before?

GINNY: No, and I'm not exactly . . . I'm not sure this is what I want.

OLDER WOMAN: Come on, what's up with you? Of course it's what you want.

GINNY: I'm not sure.

OLDER WOMAN: Look, you're wasting my time. You gave me the come-on in the club and now you're playing hard to get.

GINNY: Leave me alone.

OLDER WOMAN: Oh grow up. You know what it's all about. I'm going.

OLDER WOMAN *exits to audience.*

GINNY: Suddenly you realise you've spent your life getting away from that. That wasn't a woman, that was a male impersonator and that's not what I want. I want a woman who wants to be a woman.

DEBBIE *enters from the audience.*

DEBBIE: What are you doing?

GINNY: Looking at these papers.

DEBBIE: You don't have to do that now, do you?

GINNY: Oh, yes I do. I've got a collective meeting tonight.

DEBBIE: Oh, Ginny . . .

GINNY: I promised I'd go.

DEBBIE: I thought you promised to be here tonight.

GINNY: I'll stay tomorrow. Oh, shit, I can't tomorrow. I'll stay on Wednesday, all right?

DEBBIE: Sure you can manage Wednesday? Sure I won't be interfering with any of your other pressing commitments?

GINNY: Look, it's not funny, I've got to finish these. I stay as often as I can.

DEBBIE: And you like to know that I'll be here, whenever you decide to drop in, don't you?

GINNY: I don't expect you to be here. That's not what our relationship is all about.

DEBBIE: Relationship! Is that what we're having? I don't consider two nights a week after 11 p.m. much of a relationship.

GINNY: You have to accept me the way I am. I accept you the way you are. We have our own lives to lead. This way nobody gets hurt.

DEBBIE: I get hurt. I wait in because you say you might drop in. Why won't you move in with me? Then at least this is where you'd come back to.

GINNY: You wanna get married?

DEBBIE: Don't be sarcastic, Ginny. I want to spend more time with you. I find it really frustrating the way it is.

GINNY: I need my own place. Suppose I moved in. What if I wanted to spend the night out? You'd be upset.

DEBBIE: Of course I bloody would.

GINNY: Well I can't deal with that right now.

DEBBIE: You could make an effort. (GINNY *tries to touch* DEBBIE.) No. When you kiss me I can't think straight! (*Laughs.*) We've got to talk about this.

GINNY: Well, I haven't got time to talk about it right now.

DEBBIE: Great. You see, whenever we get on to this subject, you get up and leave. It's always what you want to do. Take tonight. You come for a meal, then you piss off to your meeting.

GINNY: Are you serious?

DEBBIE: For all your feminist theory . . .

GINNY: Go on.

DEBBIE: Well you treat this place like a hotel. How do you think I feel?

GINNY: I never really thought about it like that.

DEBBIE: Well start thinking about it. It's just the same as if you went to the pub with your mates. I'm left in the same situation.

GINNY: Look, I'll get away early. I'll come back tonight.

DEBBIE: I won't count on it.

GINNY: I don't want to lose you. I don't want us to split up, Debbie.

They kiss.

MRS ALLAN *enters from the audience.*

MRS ALLAN: I hear couples are back in fashion again.

JULIE: Oh, the arbiters of sexual fashionability are proclaiming again, are they?

GINNY: Well, when I was involved very happily in a monogamous relationship, I was informed of my error, emulating male/female mores. Get out, get out, was the cry. Destroy the coupling system.

MRS ALLAN: So what happened?

GINNY: I discussed the situation very sensibly with the woman I was living with. Gradually we decided we weren't monogamous. But in practice we realised we both experienced all sorts of nasty feelings like jealousy and possessiveness when either of us slept with anyone else.

JULIE: Did you come to some sort of understanding?

GINNY: Of course, we're both very rational women. Jealousy shouldn't be allowed to ruin our love. People aren't naturally monogamous, we decided. We would try to cope.

MRS ALLAN: And?

GINNY: I've just heard that monogamy is in. You see, men aren't faithful to one woman. The old 'be faithful' syndrome is an easy way of preventing women from going outside their marriages, while men, under the guise of office lunches, 'working late, dear' or company business in Jersey can screw away to their heart's content.

MRS ALLAN: So.

GINNY: So lesbians should be faithful to one woman, that is, one at a time. I don't think they meant for life. Or did they?

MRS ALLAN: You mean?

GINNY: I mean that rather than sleeping around, which is simply imitating man's oldest perk, we should be relating, sexually that is, to just one woman at a time, so I've heard.

JULIE: Aren't you rather denigrating the women's movement by bringing it down to this sexual perspective?

GINNY: That's out as well.

JULIE: What is?

GINNY: Thinking of sex as dirty or degrading. Get with it, sister!

THREE OTHER WOMEN *stand and explain why one should not be openly gay.*

FIRST WOMAN: I've lived with the same woman for nine years and we do think of ourselves as married. Why do they tell us we're supporting a system that puts us down? That's rubbish, we are accepted. Why shouldn't I enjoy having a drink at the pub with the boys? And I always take Val, Sunday lunchtimes. What's wrong with being accepted as one of them, being treated just like anyone else? If that's the way I want to live? If the woman I live with wants to cook for me and wash my shirts, why shouldn't she? Val – that's my other half – has two kids from when she was married. She gets a bit of alimony from her husband, when the authorities can find the bastard, but it's not worth much, so she needs someone who won't let her down. I don't really understand this equality bit, they all look alike; who do you call 'mate' and who do you ask for a dance? Bread and bread, I mean what do they do? People say I pretend to be a man, but I don't feel like a woman. The point is, you see, I'm not really gay.

SECOND WOMAN: I remember once being interviewed for promotion at work. I dressed in my nicest clothes, I knew the interviewers would be male. After I sat down I relaxed a little, but when I heard the first question I nearly collapsed! Did I have any intention of marrying within the next few years, or was I engaged or committed in any way? 'Of course not,' I replied faithfully. The definite tone of voice worried them because with great concern in his voice the chairman of the panel asked me about my social life. 'But do you go out?' he pressed, eager to know. 'Of course,' I jumped in, 'but I play the field, as it were. I know numerous men.' The air cleared of that awful tension, they all smiled broadly, nodded their heads in approval and told me they had to make sure that the women who gained promotion weren't just going to waste the firm's time by getting married and chucking the job. They were obviously impressed by my attitude to work. Three days later I received news of my promotion.

One day a week I go to the Gates, they know me quite well now and I've made quite a few friends there. I don't invite them to my flat and they don't ask me. We just meet once a week for a drink, a dance or two and a chat. They're girls like me in secretarial or administrative work but I wouldn't be seen with them in the street. Oh, we're not like those homosexuals who yell about it from the rooftops. I think it's nobody's business but my own. I don't think it's relevant or necessary to talk about it, certainly not to politicise. I don't want to lose my job or get chucked out of my flat. I have straight friends, I don't want to alienate them. I'm very happy as I am, I mind my own business. That's not being in a closet – that's common sense.

THIRD WOMAN: You have to understand, we don't want to be like this – different, strange, odd. We didn't choose to be like this. Given the chance we'd be heterosexual, most homosexuals would rather be straight, normal . . . accepted. You see, all we want to do is live ordinary lives like anyone else. What we want is to be able to work and live happily together without anyone bothering us. Can't you just let us sleep, eat and love the way we want to? We can't help the way we are. We'd much rather be like you, so please don't punish us for being different. We look just like anyone else, don't we? You can't identify us in the street, can you? Well, not unless we dress or behave in a way that might give us away. We do try to be inconspicuous. Of course there are some gays who try to imitate the opposite sex, but most of us don't. The way I feel is that if anyone knew I was gay it must be because I was butch in some way. If that ever happened I'd . . . I don't know what I'd do, I just couldn't go on. I'm not ashamed of being a lesbian, of course, I just don't want anybody to know.

GINNY: A woman stopped me in the street, a stranger, although I'd noticed her sometimes in the launderette or doing her shopping. She came up to me as I was walking home. 'I'm sorry to bother you,' she said, 'I notice you a lot around here, I see you walking with your friend, you wear that badge. I've often wanted to talk to you but I never . . .' I invited her home. She couldn't stop talking, there was so much to say, things she'd never been able to tell anyone. The woman cried. She felt so emotional about being with another woman who was listening to her. She was lonely, she was confused. What could I do? Should I give her the advice I'd been given? Clubs, organisations, 'befriending societies'? I realised I had in fact made my sexuality public property. By wearing a badge I had invited this woman's approach, made it possible for her to talk with me.

What those women have just said seems to make perfect sense – but how long can you keep up the pretence? And why should you? *You are still looking at a screaming lesbian and I'm looking right back at you!*

Blackout.

Any Woman Can

I wrote *Any Woman Can* in 1974. I was 21 and working as a Stage Manager at the Kings Head Theatre Club in Islington. We had a play running at the time called *Kennedy's Children* by homosexual playwright Robert Patrick. The play was a series of monologues by characters in a bar all re-living their experiences of America in the 60s. They did not inter-act but the play was as moving, as dramatic and as funny as anything I'd seen which used more traditional forms of theatre. Robert encouraged me to write and if I could only write in 'streams of consciousness', speaking directly to the audience in an almost conversational way, then *Kennedy's Children* showed me it was perfectly valid to do so. I didn't write because I felt I had a writing skill, I wrote because I felt a deep frustration at not being able to express those things that were most dear to me. *Any Woman Can* was my 'coming out'.

The first production of the play took place for just one night in November 1975. I had become close friends with fellow theatre workers Kate Crutchley and Mary Moore and I showed the first draft of the play to them. I'd known secretly that they were . . . well, you know . . . like that . . . but it wasn't ever spoken about. I just knew. Well, you do don't you.

We put together a small production and performed it at the Haymarket Theatre Leicester, as part of a Women's Theatre Festival in the Studio Theatre. Miriam Margoyles played the lead, and we were ecstatic. It worked, basic and crude as it was!

Early in 1976 Drew Griffiths and Gerald Chapman, founder members of Gay Sweatshop invited us to put on *Any Woman Can* during the Gay Sweatshop lunchtime season at the ICA, in those days a radical Arts Centre. They also invited us to join the company, the first women to do so. That was my second 'coming out'. Gay Sweatshop was Britain's first professional gay company and to be involved with them was to devote your life, on and off stage, to being a professional lesbian. We learned a lot during that season. We realised that even radical and alternative theatre was providing few if any positive images of gay men and lesbians, and the queues winding down the Mall and into the ICA told us that we were doing something new and desperately needed. I also learned that we should have used an all-lesbian cast in the ICA production. Later we would make a political choice only to employ gays and lesbians. This was to be our theatre company and the theatre company for our community. I certainly didn't mind who came to see our shows, but one thing was clear – it was for homosexuals first and the rest of the world second. We spent the rest of 1976 touring *Any Woman Can* and sometimes meeting up with the men and performing a double bill with *Mister X*, their first self-penned show. All the company were lesbians and I know that we took an almost defiant pride in our uncompromising stand that only lesbians could play lesbian parts. *Any Woman Can* has many flaws, amongst them that it lacks dramatic cohesion and perhaps more importantly, that it lacks a feminist analysis on issues such as class or race. In fact the play contains little political analysis. At that time I simply did not see my lesbianism as part of a wider liberation struggle. *Any Woman Can* treads, rather innocently, through relationships, 'coming out', clubs, a bit of discreet sex, a bit of indiscreet sex and betrays my white middle-class origins very well. But my innocence didn't last long. I became politicised through working with Gay Sweatshop, at one point becoming a separatist and refusing to work with the men. And my radical feminism emerged throughout those years of touring with Gay Sweatshop.

The most exciting and I think the most pleasurable memories are of the women outside London, who, perhaps, lacking the support of a big city community, would come to see our shows with an enthusiasm and generosity that I have rarely since encountered in the relationship between a theatre company and its audience. After seeing our show, women would literally come up to us and say 'I've never met another one . . .'. And it's for those women *Any Woman Can* was written. And for them it was vital that we didn't turn round and say 'Sorry love, I'm just playing a part'. *Any Woman Can* was written 13 years ago and for that I ask indulgence! All the women who worked on it contributed, not just in their performance, but in improvements to the script and in the discussions after performances which were an integral part of our work process. Despite my own and other people's criticisms I still think this play is relevant. Have things really got so much better that we don't need to have a constant affirmation? I certainly do.

Jill Posener
1987

List of plays performed by Gay Sweatshop

1975/6   *Mister X* by Roger Baker and Drew Griffiths

1976   *Any Woman Can* by Jill Posener
         The Fork by Ian Brown
         Randy Robinson's Unsuitable Relationship by Andrew Davies
         Stone by Edward Bond
         Indiscreet by Roger Baker and Drew Griffiths
         Jingleball (Parts 1 and 2) by the company with Drew Griffiths
         Age of Consent devised by the company

1977   *Care and Control* devised by the company, scripted by Michelene Wandor

1977/8   *As Time Goes By* by Noel Greig and Drew Griffiths

1978   *Jingleball* (revival)
         Iceberg devised by the men and women of the company
         Warm devised by the men of the company
         What the Hell is She Doing Here? devised by the women of the company

1979   *The Dear Love of Comrades* by Noel Greig, with a musical score
             by Alex Harding
         I Like Me Like This by Sharon Nassauer and Angela Stewart Park
         Who Knows? by Philip Timmins, Sara Hardy and Bruce Bayley

1980/1   *Blood Green* by Noel Greig and Angela Stewart Park

1983/4   *Poppies* by Noel Greig

1984/5   *Telling Tales* by Philip Osment

1985   *Poppies* by Noel Greig (second production)

1985/6   *Raising the Wreck* by Sue Frumin

1985   GAY SWEATSHOP TIMES TEN FESTIVAL, during which the following
         were given rehearsed readings:
         England Arise by Carl Miller
         Ties by Tasha Fairbanks
         Meet My Mother by Michelene Wandor
         Lifelines by Nicolle Freni
         Aliens and Alienists by Rho Pegg
         Dreams Recaptured by Martin Humphries
         Hitting Home by Diane Biondo
         Pinball by Alison Lyssa
         Angle of Vision by Deborah Rogin
         Education Part 1 by Ibo

1985/6   The following were produced as GSX10 productions:
         Skin Deep by Nigel Pugh
         Julie by Catherine Kilcoyne
         More by Maro Green and Caroline Griffin
         Compromised Immunity by Andy Kirby

1987   GAY SWEATSHOP TIMES TWELVE FESTIVAL, during which the
        following were given rehearsed readings:
        The Gleaners by Maria Aristarco
        Seven Seas by Adèle Saleem
        This Island is Mine by Philip Osment
        Twice Over by Jackie Kay
        Where to Now? by Martin Patrick
        The Legend of Bim and Bam by Matthew Audley
        A Crossed Line by Christopher Eymard
        Canada Flash by Paul Doust

DOUBLE VISION

Double Vision was devised by the Women's Theatre Group and presented on a national tour which began at the Old Bull Arts Centre, Barnet, on 13 October 1982, with the following cast:

NARRATOR/MUSICIAN	Joanne Richler
CHUM	Adèle Saleem
SPARKY	Hazel Maycock

Directed by Libby Mason
Designed by Penny Fielding
Original music and lyrics by Joanne Richler

Note: *The music for* Double Vision *may be obtained by writing to Joanne Richler, c/o Leigh Music Centre, King Street, Leigh, Lancs. WN7 4LJ*

In the original production, both the songs and the narration were performed by Joanne Richler.

SONG: *'Like Magnets'*

We share many things
It's obvious in a way
Always the same
But somehow different

Like the reflections of a candle
Held up to a mirror
It's opposite, it's slightly changed
But its reality is the same

So we travel together
Like parallel lines
Pushing and pulling
Like Magnets.

NARRATOR: You see there were these two friends who quarrelled over politics.

SPARKY: You don't think pornography is violent enough to warrant direct action?

CHUM: Yes, yes, I do.

SPARKY: Then there's no problem.

CHUM: There is a problem. I don't actually agree with this kind of action, and my getting involved in some criminal action can't possibly benefit either of us. I do not agree with the way you're going about it.

SPARKY: So what's your way? What are you doing about it?

CHUM: That's not what we're talking about.

SPARKY: What precisely are you doing about it, that's all I need to know. It's not a very difficult question, or am I explaining myself badly? Okay, we know so far that you support our aims – in theory at least – and you are in favour of direct action. Does that mean you don't personally use or buy skin magazines? Is that your contribution?

CHUM: I'm not doing anything about it at the moment, and if I do, I won't resort to terrorism.

SPARKY: No, you'll write a book about the effects of pornography in our society so that everyone can see how aware you are, and how much you care, and how badly you want to change the world we live in. Meanwhile some poor sod cares so much she takes all the risks, and all she gets from shits like you is moral indignation. I hope your book sells well.

CHUM *turns and walks away.*

NARRATOR: So there were these two women. Chum would have liked to say that they were friends, but Sparky always described Chum as her ex-lover. 'That's what she was,' Chum would have replied, 'but not all that she would like to be or indeed should have been.' Anyway, suffice it to say that there were these two women who seemed to be similar to outsiders but who saw things in a very different way. 'It was ludicrous that they had ever got together in the first place,' Chum would say with a wry smile – to which Sparky always added: 'That's the way the cookie crumbles.'

The Meeting

SPARKY *is playing pool. A* WOMAN *enters, and goes to* SPARKY.

CHUM: Do you mind if – can I talk to you for a minute?

SPARKY: Course you can, no trouble. (I think I want me mum.)

CHUM: What?

SPARKY: Do you want a drink?

CHUM: No thanks. Well, a few of us are organising a march in this area, a Reclaim the Night march, in response to the number of –

SPARKY: Are you? Are you sure you don't want a drink? What do you want?

CHUM: I don't want one. I'll get you one if you like. What do you want?

SPARKY: Whisky and dry ginger please. (*To audience.*) Do you know her? Do you?

CHUM: What we want is for as many women as possible to join us on this march next Friday, and it's important that the local residents are involved and not just –

SPARKY: What's your name?

CHUM: Bryony. And that they are seen to be as concerned as –

SPARKY: Guess what mine is. Go on.

CHUM: I don't know.

SPARKY: Guess. Try.

CHUM: Do you know about the recent attacks? Have you read anything about –

SPARKY: Sparky.

CHUM: Sparky. Hello. Don't you think it's a woman's right to be able to walk the streets alone, whenever she wants to without fear of being threatened or harassed by men?

SPARKY: Yes, I do. I do think that.

CHUM: I mean have you ever been attacked for being gay and walking home with your –

SPARKY: How do you know I'm gay?

CHUM: This is a gay pub.

SPARKY: What are you doing here?

CHUM: Well if you'd listen to me you'd know I came to get you to join –

SPARKY: Did you hear that? She came in here to get me. Walked in the door and headed straight for me. Must be my after-shave, Hai Karate.

CHUM: I came to ask you if you would join the march. I personally think it's very important that women feel protected and –

SPARKY: I'll protect you.

CHUM: I don't want personal protection, I don't think it should be necessary.

SPARKY: What do you do ?

CHUM: It's not important.

SPARKY: Have you been here before?

CHUM: No. Do you think you –

SPARKY: You should've, it's nice, I like it. My turn – what do you want? I know – bartender, can I please have a Campari and soda for Olive Oyl, she's gasping. Ice and lemon: oh, and a cherry. One for you and one for me. Do you play darts? Pool? Do you know what I am?

CHUM: No. What are you?

SPARKY: I am champion arm-wrestling woman.

CHUM: Yes, I'm very impressed. You must be very strong. But not all women –

SPARKY: I am strong, shall I show you?

CHUM: No, you don't need to show me, I believe you.

SPARKY: You will not have seen anything like this ever before.

CHUM: I'm really not that interested.

SPARKY: C'mon, put your elbow on here. It'll only take a second.

CHUM: And then do you think you might take me seriously?

SPARKY: I am taking you seriously. Come on, it's good. Now keep your elbow on the table, put your arm alongside mine, grab hold of my hand, right? Now, after three you try and pull my arm over to that side. O One, two, two and five-eighths, three.

CHUM: Oh, come on, you're patronising me. You're not pushing in the right direction. Do it properly.

SPARKY: Shush.

CHUM: Are you joking?

SPARKY: Shut up.

CHUM *wins*.

SPARKY: You liar, you've done it before.

CHUM: I haven't.

SPARKY: You must have.

CHUM: You let me win.

SPARKY: I did not. Look at that, it's all flabby now. I'm not surprised you didn't want my personal protection. All right I'll come on your march then, Popeye.

CHUM: Look, I don't – we don't want support because of an arm-wrestling contest.

SPARKY: Just when you thought it was safe to go back in the bar – Popeye.

CHUM: And don't call me Popeye. Please.

SPARKY: Do you want a drink?

CHUM: No thank you. Yes, yes I do actually. I'd like a cup of coffee.

SPARKY: What do you mean?

CHUM: To drink.

SPARKY: Mmm. Come on then.

CHUM: Where?

SPARKY: For some coffee.

CHUM: What do you mean?

SPARKY: To drink.

CHUM: This is stupid.

SPARKY: Come to my house.

CHUM: What for?

SPARKY: Coffee; and then you can tell me more about this thing.

CHUM: March.

SPARKY: Right. You could give me some leaflets.

CHUM: But I've not explained it to you yet.

SPARKY: Well now's your chance. You could even get to know me.

CHUM: Yes, yes I could. But I haven't actually got much time.

SPARKY: Neither have I. Come on.

They go.

*Song: 'Getting To Know You'.
Music.*

SPARKY: What do you think?

CHUM: Yes, it's cosy, very cosy.

SPARKY: It makes no end of difference, having your own place, I find.

CHUM: Mmm, must do. Very handy.

SPARKY: Oh yes, it's handy all right.

CHUM: Now then, about this march. I want to talk to you about it.

SPARKY: Have a drink.

CHUM: All right then.

Music.

CHUM: I have a boyfriend.

SPARKY: Really, how fascinating. What does he do?

CHUM: He's writing a book on feminist criminology.

SPARKY: Sounds like he's making a bit of a nuisance of himself. I suppose you'll be wanting to get back to him then?

CHUM: Well oddly enough, I don't think I do, right now.

Song: 'Is It That Time Already?'

Listen to the music
That's here in the night
Soon it will soften
And change with the sunlight
But until it changes
There'll be music playing tonight.

CHUM: When did you first know you were gay?

SPARKY: Well doctor, it was when my mother died.

CHUM: Have you had sex with men?

SPARKY: Oh yes, but I wasn't cut out for it. Nothing happened. I've always liked women. One day I just sort of met one, and . . . Are you tired yet?

CHUM: Did you tell your family?

SPARKY: No, I didn't tell my parents I'd slept with a woman but I didn't go and tell them I'd slept with a man either.

Music.

There's nothing wrong
With late night conversation
Not much given
Not much taken
A cup of coffee
Or a glass of wine
Who cares about tomorrow
When you're feeling so fine.

The only thing moving
Is the clock on the wall
Reminding the hours that
Time will recall
And the night will be leaving
And the shadows will run away.

CHUM: Well, I've slept with a couple of women. Close friends. It was a bit of an experiment really.

SPARKY: Well no wonder it wasn't much good then. No wonder you've not been weaned off men yet. There has to be a bit of attraction.

CHUM: What do you do?

SPARKY: Eh?

CHUM: For a living.

SPARKY: Oh, I drive an ambulance. Your life in my hands.

CHUM: I bet you're very good at it.

SPARKY: Oh . . . Would you like a record on? Do you like Glenn Miller?

Music over.

CHUM: No.

SPARKY: That's good because I haven't got any Glenn Miller records. Stand up and I'll show you the quickstep. I'm very good at dancing. Who's your favourite singer?

CHUM: What's your favourite colour?

SPARKY: Do you like *Coronation Street*?

CHUM: I usually go to the Tate Gallery on Sundays.

SPARKY: I like Dusty Springfield.

CHUM: My hobby's reading.

SPARKY: Do you like a nice hot vindaloo?

CHUM: Of course I socialise with women, I enjoy their company.

SPARKY: I like sex, I like women.

CHUM: I always joined in everything.

SPARKY: You see I never could abide this having to get involved.

CHUM: Young Socialist club on a Friday night.

SPARKY: I was in love with the lady in the cake shop for three years – but now I'm in love with Martina Navratilova. Do you mind if I call you Chum?

CHUM: No.

SPARKY: So tell me about yourself.

CHUM: That would take all night.

SPARKY: That's all right.

CHUM: Shall I stay then?

Song.

The only thing moving
Is the clock on the wall
Reminding the hours that
Time will recall
And the night will be leaving
And the shadows will run away.

There's nothing wrong
With late night conversation
Not much given
Not much taken
A cup of coffee
Or a glass of wine
Who cares about tomorrow
When you're feeling so fine.

The Morning After

SPARKY: I'm coming to get you, I'm coming to get you.

CHUM: Hello. I'm up.

SPARKY: I can see you're up. Shall we go back to bed?

CHUM: Well, I'm dressed.

SPARKY: I can help you remedy that. Easy.

CHUM: I've got to go, really. I've arranged to go to a meeting.

SPARKY: Right then, I'd better put that bacon, eggs, sausages, tomatoes, mushrooms and toast in the bin immediately and come and help you.

CHUM: Well, I've got to meet Kate, my friend.

SPARKY: What's the matter?

CHUM: Nothing – I don't want to go really, but it wouldn't be fair to stay.

SPARKY: Well I don't think it's fair at all either.

CHUM: Don't go all funny.

SPARKY: I'm not. Can I see you tonight?

CHUM: Oh, I'm sorry, I'm going to see a film with my boyfriend.

SPARKY: Oh him with the whiskers. Can I come too?

CHUM: No. Look I really need to have a bit of a think.

SPARKY: What do you have to think for? You know what something feels like, don't you? Oh, you didn't enjoy yourself. I get the picture.

CHUM: I did enjoy myself, I did. I really like you.

SPARKY: If you're happy and you know it, stamp your feet.

CHUM: I just have to go now and have a think. It's all a bit – I don't quite know what's going on.

SPARKY: Frightened in case I ask you to move in? I won't.

CHUM: Well, you must feel a bit strange too.

SPARKY: No, I feel like I'd really like to see you again – like in about half an hour. Can't see you then, you're seeing the other woman. All right, I'll see you at lunchtime – if you can't make it then, well, this evening. This evening you're seeing Tricky Dicky so I'll say, 'Let the little lady go': so, let the little lady go.

CHUM: I'd rather you didn't call me little lady. It's incredibly patronising. Oh, don't freeze.

SPARKY: All right then, Big Fat Momma.

CHUM: There's nothing wrong with being fat – if the rest of the world happens to regard the perfect shape for women to conform to . . .

SPARKY: I know, I know.

CHUM: I'm going to take you to see a play on Friday.

SPARKY: Friday, Friday? I can't wait till Friday!

CHUM: It's about women and self-image. No, don't say anything.

SPARKY: You won't tell me where you're going tonight because you're afraid I might turn up there.

CHUM: I'll see you on Friday then.

SPARKY: If you tell me where you're going tonight I can think about you.

CHUM: I'll think about you too.

SPARKY: Do you want to do it again?

CHUM: No. maybe.

SPARKY: Sometime?

CHUM: I liked it, I really liked it.

SPARKY: What did you like?

CHUM: Oh, that would take too long to explain.

SPARKY: I've got time. I liked this bit and this bit and this bit –

CHUM: Yes, shh.

SPARKY: Everyone who gets up in the morning has a cup of tea. Everyone in the world. I'd think I was neglecting my duties as a hostess if I didn't make you a cup of tea. Very remiss. There you are. Tea isn't it? Tea, tea, tea.

CHUM: I know it seems awful but I'm going to go now. Because I want to and because I have to. Please don't make me feel guilty about it. It's not fair. I'll ring you.

SPARKY: What's my telephone number?

CHUM: 237 0654 – see, I memorised it.

SPARKY: I'll have to watch you.

CHUM: Now I'm going.

SPARKY: 'Course you are.

CHUM: Right then. Bye.

SPARKY: Bye. Bastard.

NARRATOR: So, there were a few slightly delicate moments of misunderstanding and misinterpretation but not as many as might have been expected. Mostly, Chum was proud of her new lover and of her old friends and she thought it only right that they should meet.

Chum's World

SPARKY: I liked it though.

CHUM: Did you really? I wanted you to.

SPARKY: You seemed very happy there.

CHUM: Yes I am. I feel good there.

SPARKY: It's only that it's completely different. I mean I think it's good you being with all those women and liking them all the time and having fun together. I think it's good.

CHUM: Would you like to join the group?

SPARKY: No, not just yet. I don't know whether I want to go. I don't feel it's quite me somehow. I like to do things I think are me. I didn't feel I quite had my feet on the ground there or something.

CHUM: All right that's fine. Thank you for coming though. You're all right you are.

SPARKY: I know. You are too if it comes to that. Marilyn's a bit much though, isn't she, with her made-to-measure boots. 'End to the oppression of the feet, Sparky! And by the way, do have a wholemeal cookie?'

CHUM: They're very good for you.

SPARKY: 'Actually I work in a bicycle repair co-op.'

CHUM: 'Two wheels are much more fun than four.'

SPARKY: 'I run a creche, bookshop, café and write a few articles for *Spare Rib* in my spare time.'

CHUM: Do you – you look like a lorry driver to me.

SPARKY: Close, close.

CHUM: I think you're right off, actually.

SPARKY: I think you're a bit of a poppet actually. Guess who this is:

SPARKY *does a funny walk.*

CHUM: My Auntie Susan.

SPARKY: Yes. Now who's this? It's that big butch Caroline. Her of the big shoulders.

CHUM: Now you're going too far, aren't you?

SPARKY: Yes, but she was a bit, wasn't she? Sunday, then?

CHUM: Tomorrow.

NARRATOR: And of course Sparky was proud of her new lover and took every opportunity to show her off to whoever happened to be around at the time. More than occasionally, Chum would make a mental note to talk to Sparky about her behaviour but more often than not she dismissed her doubts as being puritanical and slightly small-minded. Because, as we all know, Love Conquers All.

Music: 'Love is a Many Splendoured Thing'.

The Good Things 1: Playing Pool

SPARKY: Blue ball onto the red ball and into the top pocket. Blue ball into the top pocket. Yellow off the cush and into the centre pocket. Brown in the bottom pocket and back for the black in that pocket there ... Better luck next time, pal. Do you want a game?

CHUM: No, I'm all right.

SPARKY: Go on, I'm bored of playing. You can have my next game.

CHUM: No, I don't want it. You play. I want you to play again.

SPARKY: Why?

CHUM: I just do.

SPARKY: Why?

CHUM: I like watching you being good at it. Ruling the roost and showing off. I don't think I quite approve, but I do like it.

Music: 'As Long As He Needs Me'.

SPARKY: You're a weirdo. Are you still seeing Tricky Dicky?

CHUM: Yes.

SPARKY: Do you do it with him?

CHUM: No. It always was more than sex.

SPARKY: I'll buy that. Will he?

Music: 'To Know You Is To Love You'.

The Good Things 2: Chum on the Phone

CHUM: Hello, this is Bryony Ellenchild from Women Against ... Bryony: B-R-Y-O-N-Y Ellenchild. E-L-L-E-N-C-H-I-L-D yes, it is unusual isn't it. I want to confirm the route for the ... no, I'm not the secretary or the chairwoman, I'm just a member of the group, we don't have a leader ... I phoned this morning and I was asked to phone back at three this afternoon. It's now six minutes past three ... Well I suggest somebody goes and gets him from the bar. I contribute to your wage, I don't see why I shouldn't contribute a few notions as to how you can best serve the public ... I'm sure it comes as a surprise to you, but our group does consist of members of the general public. Women are a majority not a minority, and women who have been or will be victims of male violence form a substantial section of the public that you are supposed to serve ... Look, I'm sure it's not your fault and I'm sure you'd much rather be out on the streets beating the shit out of black kids. Will you please pass on to the appropriate person that unless we hear from you the march will take the route we have suggested. We are expecting about five hundred and would like to be policed by women, not men.

SPARKY: I think you're magnificent.

Music: 'To Know You Is To Love You'.

Moving In

SPARKY: Why don't you move in with me?

CHUM: Oh. I don't know. It might not work.

SPARKY: No, it might not, but then it might. You never know till you try, do you?

CHUM: No. But we'll have to talk about what our – you know – expectations and stuff are ...

SPARKY: Of course, my little poppet.

Song: 'It Takes Two to Tango'

So the relationship's been easy
no need to define your terms
then suddenly you find
you're spending less time
with your friends and/or doing
your work

the warning bells are sounding
better sit down and sort it out
this association resembles strangulation
and the gentle voice turns to a shout

don't want to be a couple
don't want to live a lie
don't want to seem
to be holding up the dream
of the happily forever or die

Don't want to be oppressive
by setting out lots of rules
That's very patriarchal, and it takes off
   all the sparkle
and the feelings will start to cool

this space must be respected
allowing lots of room
secure but open
trying to cope when
non-monogamy comes too soon

Don't want to be oppressive . . .
so how do you go about things
when you cannot buy a kit
just check up on your neighbours
and see if all their labours
have sorted out any of it

I Like The Way You Look

SPARKY: I like the way you look.
   I really like the way you look.

CHUM: Oh yes, I like the way you look
   as well.

SPARKY: Oh no. I look terrible.

NARRATOR: And moving in didn't seem
   to change anything at all. Sparky
   continued to be fun and entertaining
   and Chum carried on being slightly
   small-minded every now and then.

Sale of the Century

CHUM and SPARKY (together):
   Chicken pox!

CHUM: It eats away at your brain, all
   this, you know. You'll end up with
   nothing.

SPARKY: Shh, I'm watching. It's
   educational. Leeds United.

CHUM: Oh God, he's so patronising.
   'That's right my love'. Sexist bastard.
   I've a good mind to write and complain.

SPARKY: I'd just kick him in the goolies.
   Pterodactyl. 'Ere, I'm good at this. I
   think I should go on it. Oh, what's it

called . . . chukka! That's right! See?
Now what's she going to get? Eh,
Chum, look at that, a music centre for
twelve quid? Not bad. We could do
with one of those.

CHUM: You know what you are, don't
you?

SPARKY: What?

CHUM: Boogeois.

SPARKY: Don't be dirty.

CHUM: *Taming of the Shrew*,
Shakespeare. Sexist crap.

SPARKY: Oh that's not fair, there wasn't
any Women's Liberation then. He
wasn't to know, poor sod.

CHUM: That's no excuse.

SPARKY: Oh I say, a cocktail cabinet.
Ohh, do you get her thrown in? Not
bad for fifteen quid.

CHUM: Do not objectify your sisters.

SPARKY: You do – you just pretend not
to so you can get away with it. I know
you.

CHUM: Martin Luther King.

SPARKY: Dressage.

CHUM: Oliver Twist.

SPARKY: Kneecap.

CHUM: Zimbabwe.

Both cheer.

SPARKY: We make a great partnership,
don't we?

NARRATOR: So it wasn't as if they
didn't carry on having fun. Was it that
the fun took a more serious role?

Space Invaders

SPARKY: I'm bored.

CHUM: Are you? I'm busy.

SPARKY: What are you doing?

CHUM: Working. What are you doing?

SPARKY: Nothing.

CHUM: You're lucky.

SPARKY: Shall I put something on?

CHUM: Yes, that would be nice.

SPARKY: What shall I put on? I know.
'Somewhere in the Night'.

CHUM: No, no, I meant something in the kitchen.

SPARKY: Oh. All right. I'm always cooking. There you are.

CHUM: Lovely, thank you.

SPARKY: What are you reading?

CHUM: About this peace action – Nagasaki Day protest.

SPARKY: What did they do?

CHUM: They all died.

SPARKY: What?

CHUM: Died. They all pretended to die, to remind people of Nagasaki and draw attention to the fact.

SPARKY *thinks. And 'dies'. Runs from wall to wall. No response.*

SPARKY: Oh, come on, you've been reading that for ages. Should I help you?

CHUM: In a minute.

SPARKY *is a dog. Howls. Pirouettes.* CHUM *watches. Claps.*

Yes, very good. Excellent. Do you think you could be a teeny bit quieter now?

SPARKY: I don't know what to do.

CHUM: What's the matter with you? What did you do before I lived here?

SPARKY: I don't know. I can't remember. But I'm more bored now that you are here.

CHUM: You must have done something.

SPARKY: I know but I want to do something with you.

CHUM: Well you can't. Why don't you read a book – sorry, magazine? Watch television. Write something. Write a letter.

SPARKY: I don't want to.

CHUM: Well, I can't help you then.

SPARKY: I think I'm bored because you're here. I need you to look at me all the time.

CHUM: All right. I'll go out. It's your house, I'll find somewhere else to work. I'll go to the library.

SPARKY: Can I come?

CHUM: No.

SPARKY: Oh please don't go out, please. I'll – just tell me what to do.

CHUM: Anything. Do anything. I don't care what it is. Read this.

SPARKY: What's it about? And what am I looking for?

CHUM: It's about the peace camp and you're not looking for anything, you're just reading it.

SPARKY: And then will you test me on it?

CHUM: No, you can test yourself.

SPARKY *reads.*

Do you mind sitting over there?

SPARKY: Why?

CHUM: Because I can hear you.

SPARKY: I've not said anything.

CHUM: No, I know, but I can hear you. You're never still are you? I can hear your mind flying around. Do you know what I mean? You're not quiet are you?

SPARKY *walks away.*

Where are you going?

SPARKY: To have a wank.

CHUM: Well, don't make a noise.

SPARKY *looks at a wall. Watches it. Begins to measure.* CHUM *watches.*

What are you doing? Sparky? Sparky, what are you doing?

SPARKY: Sshh, I can't concentrate.

CHUM: Well, just tell me what you're doing.

SPARKY: In a minute, after I've finished this.

SPARKY *continues to measure.*

CHUM: Do you want me to help you?

SPARKY: No, no, you get on with your work.

SPARKY *continues to measure.*

CHUM: I don't want to.

SPARKY: Don't you? Oh dear . . .

NARRATOR: It wasn't even that they didn't see each other's point of view, or even start to absorb a little of each other's worlds.

Inspiration

SPARKY: I saw this thing on the telly.

CHUM: What?

SPARKY: Those women outside the missile base.

CHUM: Oh? You mean the women's peace camp?

SPARKY: Yeah. It was awful. They were just sitting there in front of the gates and the men walked right over them. Treading on their hands. I feel terrible.

CHUM: Why don't you do something about it, then?

SPARKY: What?

CHUM: Go and join them on the peace camp.

SPARKY: I'll feel silly.

CHUM: No you won't. They need more drivers. You won't feel silly.

SPARKY: Will you come?

CHUM: No, I can't – too much to do. You go, you can borrow my tent. You'll be all right.

SPARKY: Okay then.

NARRATOR: In some ways, outside events started to make things much clearer.

Music.

The Homecoming

SPARKY: I'm home.

CHUM: I can see.

SPARKY: Oh – Chum – Chum – Chum. It's wonderful, where have you been?

CHUM: Here – here – here.

SPARKY: I'm starving. Is there anything to eat?

CHUM: Of course there is. Especially for you, made with love and lust and a single kiss.

SPARKY: Oh good. You've got to come down with me. We need more women and I'm going back at the weekend so you can come then.

CHUM: Do you like it?

SPARKY: I love it – you must come.

CHUM: I mean your dinner.

SPARKY: Yes I do. Will you, will you come?

CHUM: *You* liked it then?

SPARKY: I loved it, I want to marry it and I didn't miss you a bit, I was too busy.

CHUM: Good, I'm proud of you. I've done stacks of work, and I've managed to get quite a lot of my own stuff done too.

SPARKY: What do you mean?

CHUM: Writing.

SPARKY: Oh yeah, good. What do you think then?

CHUM: What about?

SPARKY: You're not listening – about coming to the peace camp with me.

CHUM: I'm fine, thanks.

SPARKY: What?

CHUM: Just in case you wondered how I've been while you've been away. Do you want to know what I've been doing?

SPARKY: Yes, what have you been doing?

CHUM: Are you sure you're interested?

SPARKY: Positive. Are you all right?

CHUM: Yes. Well, let's see, what have I done? I've painted the skirting boards and window frames. I've written some things and – I've built a cupboard.

SPARKY: Good, that's really good.

CHUM: Yes, I'm quite pleased with myself. Would you like to have a look at the pieces I've written, I think you'd be able to –

SPARKY: Oh not now. After eh? I want to tell you about –

CHUM: Yes, I meant later on, not immediately. So what have you been doing then? What did you do all day?

SPARKY: I can't tell you how good I felt, I don't mean virtuous, but –

CHUM: What did you do when you got up in the morning?

SPARKY: Are you testing me?

CHUM: No, I'm interested.

SPARKY: Okay, well, first of all I'd get up and have a look round to see if anyone else was up, and then either me or somebody else –

CHUM: Where did you sleep?

SPARKY: In a caravan –

CHUM: So, you didn't use my tent, then?

SPARKY: No, it doesn't matter – someone would make some tea and breakfast for whoever wanted it, and then if anything was already planned we'd get on with organising it, and if not –

CHUM: Like what?

SPARKY: Like what what?

CHUM: What sort of things did you organise?

SPARKY: Well, we staged a number of blockades. What we'd do is we'd –

CHUM: Blockading what?

SPARKY: The entrance to the site.

CHUM: What for?

SPARKY: So that people couldn't get in. So we would disrupt their day and make them think what they were doing and why we were there.

CHUM: And were you successful?

SPARKY: Of course we were. They couldn't run us down, could they? They're only allowed to use bombs. What do you mean successful?

CHUM: What did you do if you hadn't planned anything?

SPARKY: See, we'd spend quite a lot of time talking to people who called in. Told them what we were doing there, and there's loads of people interested, you know, all sorts of –

CHUM: Sounds like a free camping holiday.

SPARKY: It's not at all. There's no 'facilities'.

CHUM: Are they well organised?

SPARKY: What do you mean?

CHUM: Well, do they make sure that the newspapers are there to cover all the action?

SPARKY: Sometimes they're there.

CHUM: And do they make sure the local people know what's happening and keep them informed? Because getting their support would be –

SPARKY: You're mad. Of course we do. What's the matter with you? Why do you keep trying to pick holes in what we're doing?

CHUM: I'm not.

SPARKY: You are, you're trying to put it down all the time.

CHUM: I'm not, I'm making suggestions.

SPARKY: You're not, you're getting at me.

CHUM: No, I think it's very admirable of you, risking imprisonment and chatting to your admirers.

SPARKY: What the fuck have you done? Nothing. Built a cupboard – how startling. I don't think it's been done before. And you've written something. Surprise, surprise.

CHUM: I only wanted you to show some interest in what I'd been doing.

SPARKY: I did.

CHUM: No you didn't. You were so full of what you'd been doing and where you were going next that you forgot to ask.

SPARKY: So I'm being punished for feeling good.

CHUM: It's not that. It's just that I've been doing things that are important too. At least they are to me.

SPARKY: Like what?

CHUM: I've told you.

SPARKY: Oh yeah.

CHUM: When are you going back to the camp?

SPARKY: I'm not sure.

CHUM: I thought you were going at the weekend.

SPARKY: I've not decided yet.

NARRATOR: And after a time, who's to say they weren't coming to grips with their problems.

Music.

The Bad Things: Balloons

SPARKY *is blowing up balloons.*

CHUM: What are you doing?

SPARKY (*gasping*): I don't know! I just found myself with this thing in my mouth. Ugh! What is it? What does it look like I'm doing?

CHUM: Blowing up balloons.

SPARKY: Good.

CHUM: Okay. Why are you blowing up balloons?

SPARKY: Well, I'm not actually blowing up very many. I was rather hoping you'd walk in through the door, like you did, and say 'Oh my darling let me help you with those', like you didn't.

CHUM: Sparky, it's five thirty. We've got people coming round at seven. Why are you blowing up balloons?

SPARKY: I just saw them and thought it'd be nice, you know, brighten everything up, make it more . . .

CHUM: Normal.

SPARKY: Well, homely.

CHUM *and* SPARKY (*together*): Christmassy.

CHUM: Oh my God.

SPARKY: Look, the turkey's in the oven . . .

CHUM: What about –

SPARKY: And I've made a nut roast for Judy and Anna. See, I don't miss a trick. Why don't you come over here and give me a huge smackeroony, then you can come and help me with these for twenty minutes, no more! And then go and lie in a hot bath while I put these up. I might even wash your back if you play your cards right.

CHUM: All right.

SPARKY: That's my little poppet.

CHUM: You should have got one of those little hand pump things. They don't cost much.

SPARKY: Well, I didn't, did I.

CHUM: It would have saved a lot of time and energy.

SPARKY: All right, I'm sorry I didn't get one – I didn't think.

CHUM: No, you didn't, did you? Look, you're not breathing right. You should breathe deeply, right down here, then let it out evenly.

SPARKY: What makes you the bloody expert on breathing?

CHUM: Yoga, actually.

SPARKY: Look, I can't do it now – I can feel you looking at me, waiting for me to do it wrong. Why don't you just do it your way and let me do it my way?

CHUM: Because your way is, objectively speaking, inefficient.

SPARKY: Right then. Why don't you decide the best way of doing it, objectively speaking, of course, then write a paper on it and give it to me to read and I'll follow your instructions. You do, you think you know best about everything, don't you?

CHUM: Well at least I think. You just barge headlong into things and expect me to sort it out after.

SPARKY: I don't expect anybody to sort out anything for me. That's your problem. You have to stick your nose in all the bloody time.

CHUM: I stick my nose in? God, you never leave me alone. I can't do anything without you crowding me out. I have to go out to get any privacy.

SPARKY: Why do you hang about then? Why do you stay with me? Am I good for your image?

CHUM: Don't be pathetic.

SPARKY: Don't patronise me!

CHUM: I'm not patronising you, you stupid –

SPARKY: You are!

CHUM: I'm not!

SPARKY: You are!

CHUM: I'm . . . oh this is mad. Look, let's just calm down, get everything together for tonight, and then we can talk tomorrow when we're on our own.

SPARKY: What are we supposed to talk about tomorrow?

CHUM: About what's just happened.

SPARKY: What's to talk about? We had a row. Everyone has rows.

CHUM: Yes, but it was about things, important things in our relationship that need sorting out.

SPARKY: We get on each other's nerves sometimes, that's all.

CHUM: So what are we supposed to do? Wait until we're driving each other completely mad, then split up, never speak to each other again, and look for someone else to drive us crazy, and so on and so on . . . I don't believe it has to be like that. I think we can work at changing our relationships just like we can work at changing society. I mean most of what we do to each other is just what we've absorbed from a heterosexist –

SPARKY: I think I've heard this speech before.

CHUM: Why do you have to denigrate –

SPARKY: What does that mean?

CHUM: Put down. Why do you have to put down any attempt I make to think or express anything remotely resembling an idea?

SPARKY: All right, all right, let's talk about it now.

CHUM: We can't now.

SPARKY: Why not?

CHUM: What about the others? They'll be here soon.

SPARKY: They can join in. They'd love it. We can have a meeting about it. A feminist Christmas!

CHUM: All right, let's do it like this. Let's tell each other rationally, not emotionally, what we can't stand about the other, and how we'd like each other to change. You start. Oh, and we're not allowed to reply.

SPARKY: I don't like you being all superior and thinking you know best all the time.

CHUM: I don't like the fact that you don't think about what you're doing. You just do it.

SPARKY: I don't like you always thinking about everything, so there's nothing left to find out.

CHUM: Sometimes I don't like you being so facetious. Making a joke out of everything so it's difficult to be serious.

SPARKY: I don't like the way you think I don't understand anything.

CHUM: I don't think that!

SPARKY: Uh uh!

CHUM: I don't like the way you take up so much space. Sometimes I find you really overbearing.

SPARKY: I don't like you being all virtuous and sneering and criticising me all the time.

CHUM: That's the same as you said before.

SPARKY: Well, I don't like it a lot.

CHUM: I don't like the way you sometimes touch me like I was a little doll and call me names like 'poppet'. Specially when you do it in public.

SPARKY: I don't like the way you go all untouchable sometimes. I don't like it when you won't let me touch you. (*Pause.*) I think I've run out. What do we do now then?

CHUM: Well, we think about what the other person's said, and if it's reasonable or not, and then we try to change.

SPARKY: When?

CHUM: From now onwards I suppose.

SPARKY: Right, let's go back and do that bit of our lives again.

CHUM: What do you mean?

SPARKY: Do you coming in, and seeing me with the balloons. Only we've both got to change.

CHUM: Don't be silly.

SPARKY: Uh uh!

CHUM: All right.

CHUM *goes out.*

SPARKY: Okay, you can come in now.

CHUM *re-enters.*

CHUM: Oh. That's a good idea. You are clever.

SPARKY: Thank you.

CHUM: Shall I give you a hand?

SPARKY: Yes, that would be nice. I'll move over here, shall I? That'll be your space, and this'll be mine.

CHUM: Okay, but give me a cuddle first.

Balloon blowing.

Gosh, that's a good way of blowing, I think I'll do that too.

Puff, gasp.

SPARKY: That's not fair, that's cheating.

CHUM: I know, but you can't stop yourself thinking things, can you?

SPARKY (*picking her up*): No you can't, can you?

CHUM: Put me down. You know I hate you doing that.

SPARKY: Yes, I do know you hate it. But I think you like to hate it, you see. And you'd really hate it if I didn't do it, 'cos you wouldn't have anything to niggle about.

Song: 'Honestly'

Honesty, let's talk quite honestly
let's put aside emotion and deal with
    fact
such honesty that shows such clarity
and all the things that feelings lack

Honestly, what about the fallacy
that the truth only hurts for a moment
    in time
since the pain is pure, time is the
    perfect cure
at least I think that's the line

but how can you see more clearly
if tears obscure the view
the politics of openness
nothing hidden or left unsaid
confuse what's right with the best
    thing to do

you feel better that you've been
    honest
but better is a relative term
you know in the end it will work
    itself out
why, what else could you have
    honestly done?

Sparky Finds a Piece of Writing

CHUM: Hello, how're you? I'm absolutely exhausted. I've been traipsing round all day with these posters. I'm so glad to be home, I can't tell you. How was your day?

SPARKY: All right.

CHUM: Come and tell me about your day.

SPARKY: No, you tell me about your day.

CHUM: All right, I love our cups of tea together. It's like coming home from school.

SPARKY: Is it?

CHUM: Come and sit over here.

SPARKY: No.

CHUM: Why?

SPARKY: 'Cos I'm not keen today.

CHUM: Oh yes. Can I sit here then?

SPARKY: Okay.

CHUM: What shall we do this evening? Shall we go to the Crown and Castle?

SPARKY: No.

CHUM: Oh, that's unusual for you, not wanting to go there. You must be feeling off. Do you want to do anything? Do you want to watch telly? Do you want to sit alone? Do you want me to go out? What's the matter? You're making me really scared now.

SPARKY: Don't be scared. What kind of things do you write?

CHUM: Why are you asking me that?

SPARKY: 'Cos I don't really know.

CHUM: Why are you asking me that?

SPARKY: It might be because I don't know. It might be because it's something you do really well. You know, you might get all your things published in time.

CHUM: Have you been going through my things?

SPARKY: What would I want to go through your things for, because they're nothing to me. I've got no desire to go through your things. Have you had a good day? What's the matter with you? Why don't you talk? What's the matter with you? Why don't you talk? Fuck you.

CHUM: Have you read something of mine?

SPARKY: Er, yeah.

CHUM: You should leave things alone when you see they're mine.

SPARKY: Why?

CHUM: Because they're private. And personal.

SPARKY: Why are they private and personal?

CHUM: Because if I felt the need to show you I would do.

SPARKY: Well it was on the table.

CHUM: Well I must have left it there by mistake.

SPARKY: Did you?

CHUM: Yes. And if you're upset by it, it's your own fault, because you shouldn't have read it. Never read my writings again without asking. You've no right.

SPARKY: No, I won't. That's right.

CHUM: Well, shall we talk about it?

SPARKY: No, what for?

CHUM: Why you're upset.

SPARKY: Can't you tell me why? Maybe you can tell me why. Because you're kind of smart. You can write rhymes – I think. I think they were rhymes, I'm not sure.

CHUM: I'm not very good at rhyming and I'm not very good at writing maybe.

SPARKY: Maybe not. 'What a pretty funny alligator.'

CHUM: It's furry actually, furry.

SPARKY: 'Sparky was chops and peas
Chum was mint teas,
Sparky was juicy and chewy and tulip bulbs
Chum is enjoying the things that Sparky says and does.
Why is she so different?
Sometimes she is hated and pitied and despised.'

CHUM: Okay, don't. It's not meant to be read out loud.

SPARKY: No, why not? Fuck you, fuck you. It's good this is.
'Especially when she brings home a bloody great cuddly toy.
Ha ha says Chum.
What fun. With a sinking feeling inside. You see she would rather –'

CHUM: Tear it up. Go on, tear it up. I don't care about it at all, honestly. It's stupid. I hate it. I'm sorry. Please tear it up.

SPARKY: I don't know why if you don't like something you don't just say. What is it? I don't even know what you're writing it for.

CHUM: Because it's more to do with me that it's to do with you. I say, I say, 'Poor Sparky? Poor Chum!'

SPARKY: You're talking about me.

CHUM: Yes I know, but it's about me.

SPARKY: It's about me, you don't talk about yourself in it.

CHUM: I do, I say at the end –

SPARKY: No you don't, you say fuck all about you.

CHUM: I say it's my fault at the end.

SPARKY: What are you supposed to be, a martyr or something?

CHUM: Yes, it is a bit martyrish, I know that. I can't help it. Well, I can help it, I will help it. That's just what I feel like.

SPARKY: It's so unfair to use me.

CHUM: I know, I know it is. I'm not using you.

SPARKY: You are using me. I can't write things like that. I don't want to write things like that, I wouldn't dream of using you for anything. Especially as it's not, it's –

CHUM: You can write something about me. You can write anything about me. Anyone can write anything.

SPARKY: It's because I don't want to write things about you, and I wouldn't write things about you that you didn't know about. I mean, all right, you can tell people what I'm like, but I mean, if you're going to write it down or you're going to use it for something, it's so different, and it's things that I don't know about.

CHUM: I know, but I write it down because you're the important thing to me. I write about things that are important to me. What else have I got to write about? I haven't got anything else to write about, have I?

SPARKY: What if I'd never seen it? I'd be much better off than I am now, probably.

CHUM: No you wouldn't because I'd never be able to show you anything. It's stupid anyway. Don't read it again, please. Just give it back to me now, please. It was written in about two minutes when I was feeling something. Can I have it back now, please?

SPARKY: I don't mind the rest of it but I don't like this bit. I just feel like it leaves me out or something.

CHUM: I know it does. Sometimes you're a different person. Bet you think awful things about me.

SPARKY: Never have done and never will.

CHUM: Bet you do. You just don't write them down, that's all. So I can't tell you off about them. There's no evidence, is there? What about when you went slamming down the stairs last week – bet you were thinking horrible things about me then, weren't you?

SPARKY: No, I was being Bette Davis.

CHUM: Well, I'll write something about you as Bette Davis then, that will be better. Can't I ever show you anything without you getting upset, even if I think it's true? Do you think it's true? A bit, or even a moment?

SPARKY: Even a moment. What do you mean, a moment? I hate this jumper. It's oppressive.

CHUM: Right, you're back to normal then. Shall we go down to the pub, eh? I'll buy you a nice drink.

SPARKY: Yes, I will go, but I won't be very friendly for a while.

CHUM: All right. Come on then. I'll get pissed. Have a game of pool. It's a treat, you know I don't play pool very often. You'd better take your chance while you can.

SPARKY: I know what you're trying to do, you know.

CHUM: Yes, I'm trying to get round you. You like it though, don't you?

SPARKY: I do like it, I do.

CHUM: Come on then, you know what I'm going to do? I know what we can do later. We'll write a poem together. I'll write one line – it'll be like Consequences. Now you like that, don't you?

SPARKY: Yes, I do.

CHUM: It'll be like Consequences, only it'll be poetry. Shall I do that?

SPARKY: Right, only don't make me be too friendly now because I don't want to.

CHUM: No, I won't.

SPARKY: Right, come on then.

NARRATOR: The trouble was that the most minor disagreements seemed to take on a political weight. Outside events always had their effect on the pair's public and personal lives, but inside events had their effect too.

And Baby Makes Three

SPARKY: What's the matter with you, eh?

CHUM: I feel like crying.

SPARKY: What do you want to cry for? Oh, you have a good cry. My baby, my baby. What's the matter with you? Speak to me.

CHUM: I'm going to be a mother!

SPARKY: What?

CHUM: I'm going to be a mother.

SPARKY: Am I the daddy? What do you mean?

CHUM: You can be a mother too, if you want.

SPARKY: I don't want, no. What do you mean?

CHUM: You know Anna – she's pregnant.

SPARKY: Fucking hell. Who's the father?

CHUM: It's a friend. A gay man. They didn't do it or anything. They did self-insemination. Well Julie did it actually – put it up her, sort of.

SPARKY: What?

CHUM: The sperm! It was in a syringe, the bloke had, er, donated it.

SPARKY: I feel sick.

CHUM: Anyway, it worked. She's pregnant.

SPARKY: Good for her.

CHUM: And she's asked me if I want to be involved in it.

SPARKY: How are you going to be involved in it? Too late – she's already done it.

CHUM: No, listen, listen – she's going to have a home birth and me and Julie and Sandy are going to be there . . . she said to ask you if you'd like to be there too. Would you like to?

SPARKY: I would not.

CHUM: We're going to create a really good environment, not all clinical like a hospital . . .

SPARKY: And what's wrong with hospitals?

CHUM: We're going to make it a social occasion, and Marion, you know Marion, the radical midwife, we're hoping that she can deliver it. She's going to do natural childbirth, Leboyer . . .

SPARKY: It sounds appalling.

CHUM: You're only saying that because it's a bit alternative. I think it's going to be lovely, I'm really excited.

SPARKY: Why? What's so special about it? Oh, of course, it's the pinnacle of a woman's existence, isn't it, having a baby?

Music: 'Where Do We Go From Here'.

CHUM: . . . So how it's going to be is that all four of us are going to be involved in bringing the child up, so it's not just Anna's responsibility.

SPARKY: How? How are you going to do that? Where, for a start? Where will it happen?

CHUM: Well, that would have to be sorted out. I suppose sometimes it would be at Anna's and Julie's and sometimes at Sandy's and sometimes with me.

SPARKY: It's not coming here, no way. I don't want a baby here. I don't understand what it is that you're so thrilled about.

CHUM: I think it's really important – it's an opportunity to work out in practice some of the ideas that we talk about . . . and I think it's a challenge, to try and bring up a child without that element of possession that's so destructive . . .

SPARKY: I don't want a little baby here.

She puts her head on CHUM's *lap.*

CHUM: Are you a little baby? I could look after two little babies.

SPARKY: One here and one over there. Not two here.

Song: 'That Was A Bit Much'

What is difficult
Is the meaning
When you can't agree
That the compromise
That you're nearing
Seems like an impossibility
Where do you go from here?

CHUM: Do you mean it, really – you wouldn't want a child here?

SPARKY: Yes, I mean it.

CHUM: What if I ever wanted to have a baby?

SPARKY: Do you? You don't. When? Well, I think, if you did, it would be in a different life, a different time. It wouldn't be anything to do with me.

CHUM: I thought maybe it would be a possibility with you.

SPARKY: Oh no.

CHUM: You just want the good things, don't you? You just want to enjoy yourself.

SPARKY: Of course I want to enjoy myself, don't you?

CHUM: You don't have any sense of commitment.

SPARKY: Yes I do. I'm committed to being with you for as long as it's good for both of us. How would you do it anyway? Would you do that business with a syringe?

CHUM: No, I'd find somebody who I would like to be the father of my child and I would do it the usual way.

SPARKY: That's a bit conventional for you, isn't it?

CHUM: Well, I wouldn't have to be 'in love' with him, but I'd like him to have some part in bringing the child up. I think men should take more responsibility for children.

SPARKY: And how do I – that is we – our relationship – how does that fit into this great plan of yours?

CHUM: Oh, don't be horrid about it. It's not a great plan, it's not going to happen for ages, I don't want to have a baby now. But I do one day.

SPARKY: Why, why, why?

CHUM: Well, it's just an experience I don't want to miss out on. I mean it's a huge experience.

SPARKY: Yes, it is a huge experience. I should imagine it's an absolutely enormous experience.

CHUM: Why are you so upset? What part of it upsets you?

SPARKY: It makes everything different between us.

CHUM: Why?

SPARKY: Because I don't know what to expect any more. First of all there's this business with Anna's baby – well, I don't understand that but I suppose I could get used to it. And then you tell me that for some strange reason you want to find a suitable man to sleep with so that you can have his child. Well fuck off and do it – I hope you have twin boys.

Song.

It's catch the meaning
But can't make the leap
Can hear the words
But what's left to speak
If understanding and agreeing
Are two different worlds
Where do you go from here
Where do you go from here?

SPARKY: Okay. Um. What do you really dislike? I know, cats.

CHUM: I'm allergic to them.

SPARKY: Yes, So, suppose I said to you, I really want to have a cat. I want that close physical thing that you can get with cats and, of course, I want it to live here.

CHUM: You're just being silly now.

SPARKY: I haven't finished yet. Also, I want to look for a lover. A woman (of course it would be a woman in my case) who would help me look after the cat, and that would be a really strong bond between us – me and this other woman, that is. Don't you think you might feel a bit excluded or threatened or something?

CHUM: Why are you so anti-babies?

SPARKY: It's a physical reaction. I'm allergic to them. I have decided that I don't want to be in the role of mothering.

CHUM: You're so selfish, aren't you? You're really so selfish.

SPARKY: You've always said to me that women should take control of their own lives, and that's what I'm doing. I do not want an environment with children.

CHUM: And that's final?

SPARKY: Yes.

CHUM: No compromise?

SPARKY: No. We're all right as we are, why don't we keep it that way?

CHUM: Why are you being so stubborn?

SPARKY: It's just what you can deal with, isn't it? I'm not just being stubborn . . . it's because I've made a decision.

CHUM: Right, from now on nothing will come into our relationship except what you decide: except what's good fun. So, here we are, let's have fun.

SPARKY: Um, if you want a child to look after, I've got one. Good, eh?

CHUM: Don't be so facetious.

SPARKY: I'm not actually being facetious. I don't think she's available for you to look after, but I have got one.

Pause.

CHUM: Why didn't you tell me before? I feel like I've been making a complete fool of myself. Why didn't you tell me?

SPARKY: I must have been busy. I didn't tell you because there was no need to tell you until now.

Song.

So go so far
But no further
Because it means too much
It's this way
Or that way
Or no way at all

SPARKY: I just didn't like the way I was when I was pregnant. There was this thing inside me, but it wasn't anybody. And it was the way everyone was treating me, as if I was something to do with them, and I wasn't. I really resented people thinking they knew something about me, the way I lived; because they didn't. It's a lie that all of a sudden you belong to everyone else and you're like them. I might have been the same in that I slept with my husband sometimes, but basically I was sleeping with women – and that was all right between me and Alan, but because of how everyone else thinks, we had to keep ourselves really private.

But it's like when you become pregnant and you look like everyone else – it's like you belong to them. They assume that they know what you're like, how you live, how you feel – but they don't know the first thing. As if everyone shares the same feeling about children. You see, I don't think I want to mother anybody. I don't like things that need me that much. But because I don't, I'm supposed to have a problem about it. Well I've not. It's what other people think you are, and how they make reasons for what you are, that makes me feel separate.

CHUM: I do see what you're saying, and I think I understand your reasons for not wanting certain things in your life. But in a way it's because of what happened to you and what you felt and the way millions of women feel bad about being mothers; it's because of that that I want to try and find new ways of bringing up children. I want to try and make things different. Do you understand that?

Song.

Are the similarities too few to state
And the differences too many
It's late
Is goodbye the only thing left to do
Where do we go from here
Where do we go from here
Where to go from here

NARRATOR: They found it impossible to live together, so they decided to live apart. But that's not the end of the story. There are at least three possible and plausible endings. In the first ending, the two decided that whatever it was they had was worth preserving, or working on in some form, and they tried to practicalise their politics.

Ending 1: Meet You Monday

CHUM: Have you missed me?

SPARKY: Um.

CHUM: I've missed you.

SPARKY: I should hope so. I've not missed you, but I mean I think about you. But I've not kind of . . . Right, I've missed you then. Right.

CHUM: Would you like to see me again?

SPARKY: 'Course I would!

CHUM: Would you like to come over and see me?

SPARKY: Yeah. What d'you mean? How? Like describe what we'd do.

CHUM: Well, we could arrange that we'll try and see each other once a week or something. But I'd really like to see you.

SPARKY: Mm. You mean, make that a definite arrangement?

CHUM: I think we'd have to do that. If we didn't make the effort I think we'd just kind of not – misunderstandings would arise – we'd keep leaving it up to the other one to make arrangements, and not –

SPARKY: Couldn't we just leave it to when we both want to see each other?

CHUM: Well, that's what I think wouldn't happen. Because –

SPARKY: Well, sometimes I want to see you, so if it's all right for us to go out or whatever, and if you want to come, then we can just go, can't we?

CHUM: Yes. I suppose I think we're just not going to get round to it.

SPARKY: Well I'm saying I would do it. Do you want to?

CHUM: Yes.

SPARKY: I have another lover now, you know.

CHUM: Do you?

SPARKY: Yeah.

CHUM: Are you, er, is it going well?

SPARKY: It's all right. I won't bring her along, though.

CHUM: Can do if you like. I'd like to meet her.

SPARKY: Oh! No, I think we should just have our times to ourselves.

CHUM: Right. That's good. I feel terribly hurt.

SPARKY: You feel terribly hurt?

CHUM: I don't want to know.

SPARKY: Ha! Don't you? Oh.

CHUM: So don't go telling me about your goings on. Well, you can if you want to talk about it properly.

SPARKY: Oh thank you.

CHUM: I want to know about it now! Tell me about it.

SPARKY: Nothing much to say. It's all right. It's good.

CHUM: Right. Well. I'd like to see you Sunday.

SPARKY: Well. Sunday's difficult 'cos that's my only . . . it's best for me in an evening.

CHUM: Right. What about Monday? Would you like to come to the opening of a women's art gallery?

SPARKY: Um . . . So what would we do – we'd go to this gallery, and what?

CHUM: We'd have a drink there, have a chat to a few people, then perhaps you could come to my house for something to eat, and we can just chat.

SPARKY: All right, but let's just leave what we do afterwards open.

CHUM: Yes. I don't want to feel as though I'm just asking you to do me a favour.

SPARKY: No, I want to, I've just said I want to, right?

CHUM: Right.

SPARKY: What time?

CHUM: It's a quarter to seven.

SPARKY: So I'll meet you –

CHUM: Here's the card, with the place on it. Come there. I'll either meet you outside or you can come and find me in there.

SPARKY: Yes inside, then I'll be able to make a bit of an entrance.

CHUM: Yeah. Okay. Make it good, then.

SPARKY: Right.

CHUM: Right.

SPARKY: You'd better be there or I shall feel a right tit if you're not.

CHUM: Right.

SPARKY: Right.

NARRATOR: In the second ending they hardly ever met at all, each receding into her own world, occasionally meeting at single-sex parties or conferences.

Ending 2: Passing

CHUM: Hello, how are you?

SPARKY: Not so bad. How's yourself?

CHUM: I'm fine. Fine. Yes.

SPARKY: My 'ex'. I'm with her over there.

CHUM: She looks nice. Is she?

SPARKY: She's okay. You still living with the same lot?

CHUM: No, no – I'm in a different household now. More children.

SPARKY: Is that one yours –

CHUM: Yes, it – he is. Aren't you, sweetheart?

SPARKY: Cor, that was a stroke of bad luck.

CHUM: No, it wasn't, but I know what you mean. You all right then?

SPARKY: Just dandy.

CHUM: Yeah. Right then, I'll see you; bye. (*To her son.*) C'mon, pudding chops.

NARRATOR: In the third ending Sparky came to believe that the way forward was through direct action and that the time for talking was past, while Chum continued working methodically at her papers and poems, eventually achieving minor success as an author.

Ending 3: Drawing the Line

SPARKY: Will you sign my copy Mrs?

CHUM: Sparky Tent. Of course, what shall I put, something special? Are you one of my readers?

SPARKY: No, I'm an ex-lover in search of a famous name and a bit of financial support.

CHUM: Yes, highly amusing, but I'm afraid I fail on both counts. Listen, can we make an arrangement for later in the week. I've loads to do just now?

SPARKY: No, I need to talk to you now.

CHUM: Don't be so dramatic. What have you been up to?

SPARKY: Lighting fires.

CHUM: I hope you didn't burn your fingers.

SPARKY: No, just a lot of films and magazines.

CHUM: You what? I was being facetious.

SPARKY: We set fire to a sex shop, I'm surprised you've not heard about it – and I'm collecting for a defence fund for the women they've arrested. And we also need money to help support their families too. In addition to that, it would be a great help if –

CHUM: Wait a minute. Please stop. I don't actually want to hear any more, I'd rather not get involved. If you are in trouble personally I'll help you out, but I don't want any of this.

SPARKY: This is to do with me. I am involved; I've not been arrested, that's all.

CHUM: Do you have any idea what you're doing? Somebody could have been killed.

SPARKY: Nobody was hurt.

CHUM: They could have been, quite easily. It must have been sheer good fortune that nobody was in there.

SPARKY: We knew, we had made sure. But that's not the point.

CHUM: That is the point. That's exactly the point. It's a thoroughly useless and dangerous course of action – I won't support that kind of violence, no. The answer is no – whatever it is you want.

SPARKY: I've told you, there was no danger to anybody at all. All I'm asking you to do is publicly support our campaign. I would have thought you would have been glad to.

CHUM: Yes I am, in principle.

SPARKY: You don't think pornography is violent enough to warrant direct action?

CHUM: Yes, yes, I do.

SPARKY: Then there's no problem.

CHUM: There is a problem. I don't actually agree with this kind of action: and my getting involved in some criminal action can't possibly benefit either of us. I do not agree with the way you're going about it.

SPARKY: So what's your way? What are you doing about it?

CHUM: That's not what we're talking about.

SPARKY: What precisely are you doing about it? That's all I need to know. It's not a very difficult question, or am I explaining myself badly? Okay? We know so far that you support our aims – in theory, at least – and you are in favour of direct action. Does that mean you don't personally use or buy skin magazines? Is that your contribution?

CHUM: I'm not doing anything about it at the moment, and if I do I won't resort to terrorism.

SPARKY: No, you'll write a book about the effects of pornography in our society so that everyone can see how aware you are, and how much you care, and how badly you want to change the world we live in. Meanwhile some poor sod cares so much she takes all the risks, and all she gets from shits like you is moral indignation. I hope your book sells well.

CHUM: Don't walk away. Let me have the chance to explain the way I feel.

SPARKY: So you can 'make a stand'? Fuck off.

CHUM: I think the kind of violence you're involved with can only lead to more violence – and you're certainly not going to get any public support.

SPARKY: Stuff public support! We'd have to wait for ever if that's what we were after. We want change, so we're effecting it. Public support is what you depend on – and it shows. I was using you, admittedly, we can use what you've got. But please don't try and teach what is passed and failed. I haven't got the time.

CHUM *walks away. Music starts.*

Song: 'Like Magnets'

The expectations are so much higher
And the disappointments when they
    come
So much harder

Because of who we are
And because of this sameness
When it hurts, it hurts longer
When it's over – we're still not apart.

So we travel together
Like parallel lines
Pushing and pulling
Like magnets.

Blackout.

Double Vision

When the Women's Theatre Group started work on *Double Vision* in 1982 it was part of a season of work which was intended to examine the ways in which women have struggled through the ages to find a positive dynamic between their personal and their political lives. We wanted to give theatrical form to the slogan 'the personal is political'. The other plays in the season were *Love and Dissent*, a play about Alexandra Kollontai, and *Dear Girl*, a documentary piece about four socialist feminist friends at the turn of the century.

From the start, *Double Vision* was a totally collaborative effort. The group was anxious to give expression to its own preoccupations, passions and visions, rather than hazard a guess at what those of its audiences might be. I think, in retrospect, that we were part of a move among many political theatre workers who were becoming weary of what I call 'missionary theatre': the kind of theatre which wraps up political ideas in a wholesome and palatable form to be presented to an audience which, we assumed, was not familiar with, nor sympathetic to those ideas. On the other hand, we did not want to create 'ghetto' theatre: theatre which simply reinforces the world view of performers and audiences and leaves us all bathed in a rosy glow. What we wanted to say to all our audiences was: 'Here we are, feminists, some of us lesbians, with all our contradictions. We make ourselves vulnerable to you. Please engage with us in a generous way.' And, in the event, *Double Vision* was a piece with immensely broad and popular appeal. It played successfully not only to feminist and 'sympathetic' audiences but also to audiences in community centres and schools all over the country.

To return to the process. The earliest stage was workshops involving the whole company – the cast, the director, the stage manager, the administrators and two performers who were not, in the end, to perform the piece. Out of these workshops certain content areas were synthesised – class differences between women, attitudes towards childbearing and rearing, ideological purity, lifestyles, to name but a few!

The next stage was for the unit which would perform the play – two performers, a performer-musician and the director – to decide, through improvisations and discussions, on characters and a story. More improvisation, discussion and scripting (by all four of us) followed, with collaboration and comment at certain points from other company members.

It is this collaborative process which produced both the play's strengths and its flaws, and makes it potentially a very difficult script to work on. The script of the original production was, of course, one of the last things to emerge! So when we came to work on it *as* a script most of the foundation work, in terms of characterisation, the objectives of the scenes, the humour, had already been done in improvisation. There are virtually no stage directions in the script because the way the words were spoken and the physical pictures they created had already been invented and were familiar to all of us.

I have left the script more or less in the state to which it had evolved by the time the piece was performed because I believe it is important that it should be read as a record of the final stage of a devising process rather than as the kind of script that a writer might present to a company for consideration. Indeed I do not believe that one writer *could* have produced a script like this; its idiosyncracies are very much those of a particular group of women in a particular place at a particular time. One writer could never for example, have written Sparky's line 'I hate this jumper, it's oppressive' in the 'Sparky Finds a Piece of Writing' scene. That is a line that was very particular to the actress who improvised it and to the character she created. One writer would never have given the scenes the title headings we did. (Do not look for any significance in these headings – they were simply working titles for us in rehearsal.)

One writer might, however, have achieved greater dramatic unity, more consistency in style and structure, and might have written in a way that gives future directors and performers more clues!

The only consistency in the writing is in the songs. These were written and performed by Joanne Richler, who also created her own role as Narrator. Again, the way in which she did this was very particular to her own style, and successors might find problems giving the songs and narration the kind of Canadian Jewish irony which is her hallmark.

I do not think it very helpful to give much detail about design and staging. We went for an atmospheric set, designed by Penny Fielding, which had the bare minimum of furniture and props; there was no 'food', no 'cups of tea' etc. We used a style which allowed the performers to indicate objects in a storytelling fashion, rather than using real props or detailed mime.

Although we are proud to be in an anthology of lesbian plays, I should make it clear that the piece was never conceived as a 'lesbian' play, in that it does not attempt to offer generalisations from specifically lesbian relationships. We wanted to present a piece in which the central relationship *happened* to be a lesbian one, just as most plays 'happen' to have heterosexual assumptions, but do not purport to be 'about' heterosexuality. What we wanted to say about relationships would, we hoped, have resonance for heterosexual and gay women and men who experience the area of relationships as a significant political battlefield.

I have written at length about the thinking behind *Double Vision*, not because I wish to deter potential producers of the script (far from it) but in the hope that many readers may both see the play as a significant piece of theatrical and political history and use it as a tool for creating their own plays.

Libby Mason
1987

List of plays performed by the Women's Theatre Group

1975/6 *My Mother Says I Never Should* devised by the company
About teenagers, sex and contraception.

1976/7 *Work to Role* devised by the company
Discrimination against women in the workplace.

1977 *Out on the Costa Del Trico* devised by the company
About the strike at the Trico factory for equal pay.

1977/8 *Pretty Ugly* devised by the company
About advertising and fashion and their effects on teenage girls

1978 *In Our Way* devised by the company
About sexual discrimination

1978/9 *Hot Spot* by Eileen Fairweather and Melissa Murray
About sexual stereotyping.

1979 *Soap Opera* by Donna Franceschild
Trapped in a launderette, a group of women talk to each other about their lives.

1979/80 *The Wild Bunch* by Bryony Lavery
Sexism in a mixed youth club.

1980 *My Mkinga* by Kate Phelps
About drug-dumping in the third world.

1980/1 *Better a Live Cyril than a Dead Pompey* by Claire McIntyre and Stephanie Nun
A dramatisation of the work of Stevie Smith.

1980/1 *Breaking Through* by Timberlake Wertenbaker
About the nuclear industry.

1981 *New Anatomies* by Timberlake Wertenbaker
About Victorian women who dressed as men in order to explore the world.

1982 *Time Pieces* by Lou Wakefield with the company
An historical look at the lives of women throughout the twentieth century.

1982 *Double Vision* by Libby Mason with the company

1983 *Love and Dissent* by Elisabeth Bond
About Alexandra Kollontai and the relevance of her ideas to present-day feminists.

1983 *Dear Girl* by Libby Mason and Tierl Thompson
About four socialist feminist friends at the turn of this century.

1984 *Trade Secrets* by Jacqui Shapiro
About pornography and violence.

1984/5 *Pax* by Deborah Levy
Poetry and music about women and nuclear war.

1985 *Anywhere to Anywhere* by Joyce Halliday
A musical about the Women's Air Transport Auxiliary in the Second World War.

1985   *Witchcraze* by Bryony Lavery
        Women as witches.

1986   *Fixed Deal* by Paulette Randall
        Women and drugs.

1986   *Our Lady* by Deborah Levy
        Women and religion.

1987   *Holding The Reins* devised by the company with Alison Altman
        About the decision to have, or not to have, children.

1987   *Lear's Daughters* by Elaine Feinstein

CHIAROSCURO

Chiaroscuro was written for Theatre of Black Women and was first presented at the Soho Poly on the 19 March 1986, then on tour at the Drill Hall, the Oval House, the Cockpit Theatre in London, as well as at various community and art centres, with the following cast:

AISHA	Vinny Dhillon
BETH	Bernardine Evaristo
OPAL	Jacqueline de Peza
YOMI	Ella Wilder

Directed by Joan Ann Maynard
Designed by Helena Roden
Choreographed by Pamela Lofton
Music by Gail Ann Dorsey

Production Note
The events in the play take place now and then. All of the characters should be onstage all of the time. The actors should stay in character when singing the songs.

ACT ONE

On the floor is a grey cloth. There are two high-backed chairs painted black and two stools painted white. These are at the back of the stage unless being used. At the front left is an old wooden chest. The stage should be as free from clutter as possible. It should have the appearance of an almost empty yard. The backdrop is a montage of landscapes and odd photographs. Its main colour is pale grey.

The four women are all wearing the same outfit: an all-in-one jumpsuit made from stretchy material. AISHA and BETH's are red. YOMI and OPAL's are black. They will wear these throughout, sometimes adding something naturalistic. The suits should look stylised rather than fashionable.

When the audience enters, AISHA opens the chest. YOMI and OPAL stand and chat to each other. BETH scrutinises the audience.

On the floor facing north, south, east and west lie a photograph album, a cushion, an oval-shaped mirror and a black doll.

The four women listen to each other as if they have heard it all before.

The lights go down.

AISHA looks at her watch and decides it's time to begin. OPAL and YOMI continue chatting to each other as she talks.

AISHA: This is how we got to where we were.

> *OPAL signals to YOMI. They rush to AISHA and sweep her into the middle of the stage. BETH approaches the three MUSICIANS and asks them for instruments. They hand BETH four percussion instruments. BETH distributes them to AISHA, YOMI and OPAL. The music starts. It is soft and haunting. The four women dance, playing their percussion instruments.*

ALL (*sing*): Time changes light
  light changes time
  here we are with the dawn in the dark
  the dark in the dawn
  trying to find the words
  trying to find the words.

They sit down in the middle of the objects on the floor with their backs to each other. AISHA sits by the cushion,

BETH *by the album,* OPAL *by the mirror and* YOMI *by the doll.* AISHA *puts the cushion between her legs.*

AISHA: All this has happened before.

BETH: How often have you heard it told though?

AISHA: Last night and the night before that.

OPAL: Let's get on with it.

AISHA: Okay. I was called after my grandmother on my mother's side. It is a long, long story that can be told so short; people don't realise the years that went, nor the pain, and trying to find a precise beginning is always tough. So much is hard to place. A little hearsay goes a long way. But I heard say that my grandmother was born in the Himalayas at dawn. Her mother shrieked as she pushed her out of herself . . . (*She pushes the cushion out from between her legs.*) . . . and cried and cried. They called her Aisha.

They turn in a circle till BETH faces the audience.

BETH: I was called after my great-great-great-great grandmother on my father's side who was taken from Africa to slavery in America and raped often; who had children that were each taken from her. But, Beth was one strong woman; she was like Sojourner Truth or Harriet Tubman – a woman who made change, who was Change herself. She helped some other slaves escape to the free country that was North America.

YOMI laughs loudly.

The black people have been dispossessed, my daddy used to tell me. I only knew what possess meant; did dispossess mean not to own? My daddy told me he called me Beth because my grandmother's African name was whipped out of her. This was the name the white people gave her with welts in her black skin. He said *that* history had to be remembered too.

AISHA, OPAL, YOMI (*chanting*); For we have to remember it all, For we have to remember it all . . .

They turn again till OPAL faces the audience. She picks up the mirror and looks at it sideways.

OPAL: They had no one to name me after, so they called me after a stone. A gemstone, at least they thought me special! A stone that was both jewel and rock, that was a rainbow, changing with the light. Each time you looked at it you would see something different. They had no one to name me after so they called me Opal. At school the children teased me singing . . .

AISHA, YOMI, BETH (*sing*): . . . Opal fruit made to make your mouth water.

OPAL: They all liked those sweet insults like . . .

AISHA, YOMI, BETH (*sing*): . . . Nuts oh hazelnuts. Cadbury's take them and they cover them in chocolate.

OPAL: These were the white kids' songs. I don't really know how I got my name. Somebody in the home said it was after a very old nurse who wore opal earrings all the time. It was her idea. Call her Opal. So they say, anyway, but for all I know that could be hearsay.

The circle turns till YOMI *faces the audience. She puts the doll on her stomach.*

YOMI: My mother had a time of it with me. I just wouldn't come out! Her womb must have been too cosy for me to want to leave! She just got bigger and bigger and it seemed, she said, she would never have me, like she would be carrying me around inside her for the rest of her life. What a thought! Finally they cut her open and out I came, all six and a half pounds of me. (*She pushes the doll up in the air.*) At midnight. A midnight baby. She called me Abayomi. Apparently I never cried when they spanked me. My name is Abayomi. My mother was afraid I would never arrive. But here I am. Here I am. I surprised the lot of them.

They all rise. They follow OPAL *carrying their objects. They dance to the chest. A walking dance. As they go there,* OPAL *speaks.*

OPAL: And so it was that names were also chance things like an old woman's fancy or a mother's dream names relating to nothing specific except desire names with no heavy weight like Aphrodite or Persephone Gauri-Sankar or Tara – names hinged casually onto some instant liking. Name the nameless ones. Name the nameless ones.

They stop at the chest and peer in as if it is a wishing well.

AISHA: My grandmother Aisha gave me this. She made it. Beautiful, isn't it? I remember lots of the stories she told me whilst I sat on this cushion. It was a magic cushion. Her stories made me travel. Once she told me a true story and I stayed still.

YOMI: I remember. (YOMI *changes to* AISHA's *grandmother.*) 'Your great-grandmother was so bossy. She bossed me around terrible. I promised myself I would never do that to my children . . .'

AISHA: Yeah well, bossiness must skip a generation, 'cos your daughter bosses me around something chronic. (She don't anymore. I think that was during the terrible teens.)

YOMI: 'Life is too short, Aisha. You must just not bother with it. Get on and do what you want to do. It's hard enough for girls. Too many people wanting to hold them back. Sometimes I think if I could replay my life back again, which bits would I want to edit out and which would stay in, or better still, Aisha, which new bits . . . When you get to the end . . .'

AISHA (*interrupting her*): Please, Gran.

YOMI: 'Don't be silly. Death is as ordinary as life. When you get to the end you really wish you hadn't been such a coward. Take the risk, Aisha.'

AISHA: I didn't really know what she was on about then. But I remembered it and now the words make sense. Good sense.

She hugs the cushion and drops it into the chest, reluctantly.

YOMI (*hugging her doll*): I called this doll Amanda. Once . . .

AISHA: . . . she was walking down the street she lived in and some kids shouted . . .

OPAL: . . . Just because you're a darky doesn't mean you have to have a darky doll.

AISHA: So when she got home, she took it out of her pram and put Amanda in the airing cupboard. Every so often she guiltily pulled her out and called her names . . .

OPAL (*vindictively*): Nigger. Wog. Sambo. Dirty doll.

YOMI: Poor Amanda.

YOMI *puts the doll into the chest.*

OPAL: When I was little glass haunted me.

BETH: Everywhere she went it would be – in shops, in cars, all over the place.

AISHA: Once when she was eight she broke a small round mirror. She was so superstitious. She counted on her fingers how old she would be before she could be happy. Fifteen. It seemed *old.*

BETH: Whenever she looked in the glass she saw ghosts of old reflections. A face behind her face. Her face was a shock to itself.

OPAL *looks in the mirror once more, pulling a face. Then she puts it in the chest. She grabs the album out of BETH's hands.*

BETH: No. I don't want to.

OPAL: Come on Beth. We said *all* of us.

BETH: It's stupid anyway.

YOMI: Too late. All her old boyfriends are in here, the ones she pretends she never had. Yeah look. Photo-booth smooches and slurps.

YOMI *flicks through the album teasing BETH.*

AISHA: Let's just get on with it.

OPAL: Don't forget all her childhood friends – all white. And her mother pale and frightened-looking. As if her whole life is a surprise to her.

BETH *takes the album off YOMI and puts it in the chest. She throws off her mood and suddenly switches, turning around in a swirl. The light brightens.*

BETH: And don't we need surprises!

AISHA: All depends on which sort, doesn't it?

BETH: Like this one.

OPAL *picks up one of the stools and carries it to the front of the stage. She*

sits down. BETH *waits till she is comfortable and picks up the other stool.* AISHA *closes the chest and she and* YOMI *sit on it watching* BETH *and* OPAL.

BETH: Do you mind if I join you? (You with the changing eyes?)

OPAL *is reading.*

OPAL: No.

OPAL *continues to read.* BETH *stares at her.*

BETH (*to imaginary waitress*): I'll have a coffee, please. (Her eyes are amazing.) (*To* OPAL:) It's a lovely day isn't it? (And you are too.)

OPAL (*reluctantly*): Yeah. Pity to have wasted it shopping.

BETH: What did you buy?

OPAL: Oh just some earrings for a friend.

BETH *takes coffee from imaginary waitress.*

BETH: Thank you. (She's like a stranger that I know very well.) Do you work?

OPAL: (What is this?) Yeah, I'm a nurse.

BETH: Oh. (*Pause.*) That's demanding work.

OPAL: Yeah, you're telling me.

BETH: And hospital structures are so hierarchical, aren't they?

OPAL: Mmmnn (Listen to her! She seems to know more about them than me. (*Pause.*) Are you a student?

BETH (*put out*): No. I was once. Not that it counts for much these days.

OPAL: (Thought so.) Well you can only say that if you've got a degree under your belt, can't you?

BETH: Suppose so. (She is interesting. I wonder where she comes from.) Where are your parents from?

OPAL: I haven't got any. (I've had this conversation before.)

BETH: Oh. But don't you know anything about them?

OPAL: Nothing. I was brought up in a home in Hampshire. (I wonder if she always does this.) So what do you do now your student days are over!

BETH: I'm an outreach worker for a community centre in Haringey.

OPAL: Oh. Interesting.

BETH: (This is crazy. I don't even know . . .)

OPAL: Do you always do this then?

BETH (*vacantly*): What?

OPAL: Talk to strangers.

BETH: No. (*Laughing.*) Never, would you believe. It was just; well, I don't know how to put it . . .

OPAL (*interrupting her*): You remind me of someone I used to know.

BETH (*pleased*): Really?

OPAL: Yeah. I'm Opal.

BETH: I'm Beth. Opal? That's an interesting name.

OPAL: Yeah it is, isn't it? It's after the stone, you know, Opal.

BETH (*giggling*): Oh.

OPAL: Well! People are called after flowers. Anyhow, you think Opal's funny – I know someone called Turquoise.

BETH (*laughing*): Next it'll be Onyx!

OPAL (*suddenly*): Well it's getting on. I have to rush.

OPAL *gathers herself together.* BETH *is agitated.*

It was nice talking to you.

BETH: You too. Listen. (I must ask her before she goes.) Maybe we could go out for a drink sometime or something. (There, I've said it.)

OPAL *doesn't know what to say.*

Are you on the phone?

OPAL (*hesitantly*): Yes . . .

BETH: That's good.

OPAL *scrambles around for paper. Doesn't find anything.*

I'll write it on my hand.

OPAL: 800-2454.

BETH: Thanks. Okay, I'll ring you.

OPAL: Yeah do.

BETH: Maybe I'll ring tomorrow.

OPAL: (So soon?) Anytime.

Lights go down and then up again. They are softer. OPAL *picks up her stool and sits at the other end of the stage.* BETH *stays where she is, smiling.* OPAL *peers into an imaginary mirror.* BETH *watches* AISHA *and* YOMI.

AISHA *takes a quilt out of the chest and hands it to* YOMI. YOMI *dances with it as* AISHA *talks.*

AISHA: You see they decided it was time, right. Time to get out of the rut. Time to grab a chance. In the beginning there was the dream of decency and opportunity and education. My parents came here in 1953 to work and save and work and one day return home. They were the invited guests who soon found out they'd be treated like gatecrashers . . .

YOMI *interrupts her, holding up the quilt.*

YOMI: Whose were the hands that stitched these stitches?
In what language are these threads
Did the imagination of some strong woman
hold this thing together
has each piece belonged to a different child?
whose were the hands that stitched these stitches?
in what language are these threads?

AISHA: My Mum was a factory machinist. She was constantly sewing. Even when she didn't need to. It was like she couldn't stop. Making ends meet. Sometimes she downed the shirts and the dresses and made quilts – beautiful, angry quilts glorious with colour and pattern. All the words she never spoke stitched intricately. Sometimes when I look into her eyes, I think I see the dead dream in them. When I look at the quilts I hear her laughing – laughing at them that treat her like a child, laughing at her own boldness, laughing like she laughed at home. It makes me want to laugh when I hear them talking about *us* taking over. What do they think they've done? They've even taken over my tongue. Yet sometimes I worry, Yomi, that I'd never fit in back home. That I'd stick out a mile, or worse they'd call me English!

YOMI *takes* AISHA's *hand and leads her to the musicians as she talks.*

YOMI: The country of origin
the original country
back home, the place you came from
where roots still grow
out under moon and sun
the soil on which the past lies
the place which might attach itself
      to you
like a belonging

AISHA *and* YOMI *take a percussion instrument from the* MUSICIANS. YOMI *harmonises as* AISHA *sings.*

AISHA (*sings*): My dreams are in
      another language
my heart is overseas
a need is stretching like the water
to meet and meet and meet
I want to put it all together
these different bits of me
show them to my mother and
all my family my family

My dreams are deep as dangerous waters
my heart is beating at the rocks
a longing is spinning like a whirlpool
round and round and round
I want to travel over there
and join my past to now
be welcomed, not a stranger
for who I am and feel at home.

The music fades. The lights change. AISHA *and* YOMI *stay where they are and watch* BETH *and* OPAL. *Spotlight on* BETH.

BETH: I feel like I've met her before, you know. There's something about her that made me feel so at home. I just can't get her out of my head. She's left a warm glow all over me. (*Pause.*) I decided I was going to be celibate for two years. (*Pause.*) Maybe I should just give her a ring now. (*She picks up an imaginary receiver and replaces it.*) This is ridiculous! It's too soon. I could always ring her tomorrow. Oh, I just don't know what to do. 'Hello Opal, Beth here. I fancy you, would you like to get to know me better?' Can you imagine! She'd hang up probably. I could phone and a man might answer. I don't even know if she's got a boyfriend. I could phone and listen to the endless ring and my heart beat saying, *Answer-Opal-pick-it-up*!, and finally watch my

hand slowly put the phone back in its cradle. My head is spinning. (*Pause.*) I should have given her my number. No, that'd be worse; I'd just be sitting here like a prize ass waiting for the phone to ring.

Lights go down and up with spot on OPAL.

OPAL: I can't believe I'm feeling like this. It's crazy. I've only seen her three times and seen three very good films into the bargain! Not the sort I'd usually go and see, but when I'm with her it doesn't seem to matter what we do. It is so strange. She's a woman! This attraction is so physical. At first I thought, this isn't real. I must just admire her or something. But, last night I wanted to lean over and kiss her! I wonder if she feels like that for me? Maybe she just wants to be good friends. Wouldn't that be a laugh! Me melting away for her and her just wanting to be good mates. What would we do anyway? We'd go and see another film, maybe that *Desert Hearts* she's been telling me about. I'd go back to her place and . . . oh, I just can't imagine it. Sometimes, you just meet someone like that. (*She snaps her fingers.*) and you feel like you've known them all of your life. I feel that way with Beth. Somewhere I believe I was meant to meet her that day in that café before the sun went down and the summer slipped away.

Lights down. AISHA *and* YOMI *take the stools from* BETH *and* OPAL *and place them opposite each other in the middle of the stage.* BETH *and* OPAL *stand at either end of the stage and do the movements of a train. The* MUSICIANS *make train sound effects. Lights up.*

YOMI: It is one of those summer days that make you want to live in a country that knows how to be hot!

AISHA: Yeah right.

YOMI: Do you know, Aisha, I don't think I've seen any countryside for at least a year. It's Fabayo I feel sorry for. I don't think it's good for kids to be trapped in cities.

AISHA: She'll be all right.

YOMI: I've never left her before, you know.

AISHA: I know.

They look out into the audience.

I hope it's going to be all right.

YOMI: So do I. I hope she doesn't wet the bed.

AISHA: I wasn't talking about Fabayo, I meant the weekend.

YOMI: Well, it'll make a change. (*Pause.*) Actually, I haven't got a clue what to expect from it. Yet I'm looking forward to it. If it's disappointing, I can always blame you!

AISHA: Thanks, mate.

YOMI: I tell you what will be nice though, just having the time to choose what I want to do. Luxury.

AISHA: Do you think you'll go to the social?

YOMI: I might. It's women-only, isn't it? You've been to that kind of disco before, haven't you?

AISHA: Only once.

YOMI: What was it like?

AISHA: It was all right. Made a change not to be hassled to dance by some bloke who reckons you owe it to him 'cos he's bought you a drink!

YOMI: Wole would go mad. I can just hear him: 'an *All-Women's disco*?'

They laugh.

AISHA: Are you seeing much of him at the moment?

YOMI: Oh, you know, about every two weeks. It's enough for me! (*Pause.*) I think I'll try silk-screening. I've always fancied trying that.

AISHA: I wish I wasn't running this carpentry workshop, then I'd get a chance to go to the others.

YOMI: Aisha?

AISHA: Uh huh.

YOMI: At the social tonight?

AISHA: Yeah?

YOMI: You won't piss off and leave me alone will you?

AISHA: 'Course not. You know me.

Lights down. BETH and OPAL sit on the chest and pretend to be watching a film. In the middle of YOMI's monologue, OPAL takes BETH's hand. AISHA picks up the stool and takes it to the other end of the stage. She sits down and listens to YOMI. YOMI stays where she is. Spot on YOMI.

YOMI: I must hoover the carpet! This place looks like a tip. Honestly, you'd think a whole family lived here, not just the two of us. (*Pause.*) We are a whole family, I suppose, me and her. She took ages getting to sleep tonight. Maybe I shouldn't have gone away for that weekend. She's punishing me! (*Laughs softly.*) That was some weekend though! Mind you, some of those women were too angry for my liking. There's no need to make such a fuss! You'd think, from the way some of them talked, that they hated all men! Well, there's no point in that at all. I've known some pretty nasty women in my time. I felt so out of it, some of the time. Well, it was nice. That bit of time for myself. I surprised myself; I was good at that silk-screening lark. I think there were a lot of . . . lesbians there. That woman teaching silk-screening said some strange things. Half of them didn't even make sense. I think she was one. Judging by that disco, there are more than we know about. God. Was I shocked! I felt so naive. I've never seen two women kissing before. Long ones! Honestly! If they want to do that sort of thing there they should do it behind closed doors. And black women at that! I didn't think we produced them. (*Pause.*) Aisha didn't seem too bothered. (*She is irritated with her house again.*) I should have never let Wole paint these walls. The edges are all wonky. God! And that woman asking me if I was going to the sexuality workshop. I said to her – either you enjoy sex or you don't, what is there to talk about?

Lights down. AISHA and YOMI start to mime a game of pool. BETH watches them nearby. OPAL stands at the opposite end of the stage peering into an imaginary mirror. Lights up. The lights should follow the imaginary pool balls.

BETH (*appraisingly*): Not bad, Aisha.

AISHA: Yeah. I've just about thrashed her.

YOMI: Not quite.

BETH: I used to play pool in this pub down Dalston. The men in there used to get on my nerves.

YOMI: Why was that?

BETH: Well, they couldn't stand it if you beat them. They just couldn't take it, you know.

AISHA *is awkward and concentrates on the game.*

AISHA: Okay Yomi, let's see how you'll get out of this one.

YOMI: You're so kind.

BETH: Trouble with men is, they're really competitive. Women learn how to behave differently.

YOMI *pushes BETH out of her way to make her move.*

YOMI: Oh, I don't know about that. The women I work with are always competing with each other.

BETH: For male approval probably.

YOMI: For what?

AISHA *is exasperated.*

BETH: You've got a daughter haven't you, Yomi?

YOMI: Yes.

BETH: What's her name.

YOMI: Fabayo.

BETH: What age is she?

YOMI: Seven.

BETH: I'd like to have a child someday.

YOMI: Really? Well they're a handful, change the whole of your life. But I would never be without mine, though. Shot! Oh no. Just the black to go.

AISHA: What did I tell you?

AISHA *pots the black.*

Sorry old bean.

YOMI: Too bad, eh. Do you want to play the winner, Beth?

BETH: Okay. I'm a bit rusty.

AISHA: Do you want to break?

BETH *breaks.* YOMI *watches her critically.*

YOMI: Where are you from?

BETH: My father's from St Vincent. My mother's English.

YOMI: Oh.

BETH: And you?

YOMI: Nigeria.

AISHA (*interrupting her*): Oh come on, I must have told you both where the other was from.

YOMI: No. I don't think that was one of the things you told me about Beth.

BETH *is suspicious.*

AISHA: She's trying to wind you up.

BETH *concentrates on the game and pots several balls in succession.*

BETH (*pleased*): Not bad eh, considering I haven't played for ages. Mind you, the last time was enough to put me off pool for life.

YOMI: Why was that?

BETH: These jerks started hassling us and one of them poured a beer all over me.

YOMI: Oh dear. That must have been a bit of a shock.

BETH *pots the black. They freeze. Spot on OPAL.*

OPAL: My face was a shock to itself. The brain in my head thought my skin white and my nose straight. It imagined my hair was this curly from twiddling it. Every so often, I saw me: milky coffee skin, dark searching eyes, flat nose. Some voice from that mirror would whisper: *nobody wants you, no wonder. You think you're white till you look in me. I surprised you, didn't I?* I'd stop and will the glass to change me. *Where did you get that nose?*

AISHA, YOMI *and* BETH *unfreeze. BETH goes up to OPAL. AISHA stands near them. YOMI sits on the chest, watching.*

BETH: Do you still feel alone when you look in there?

OPAL: No.

BETH: I don't feel alone any more, either. When I first met you, you were so familiar, a dream I never expected to come true. Like seeing my own reflection. I used to feel that I was the only black lesbian in the world, you know. Serious. Just me on my tod.

OPAL: I don't like that word – lesbian.

BETH: It's a name.

OPAL: We don't need a name. What about this?

OPAL *motions to* AISHA. *AISHA starts to dance, holding imaginary earphones.* BETH *and* OPAL *watch her, laughing.*

AISHA: This is the twilight radio station. The station of this nation. Here's the wonderful smoochy song especially for Margaret, Annie sends you all her love, says she's sorry and still mad about you. (*Sings.*) 'You make my love come down.' Oooh she does.

AISHA *stops dancing, switches moods. She turns* BETH *around so that she has her back to the audience.* BETH's *body tenses and freezes.*

(*To* OPAL:) She first thought she might be a lesbian at school. She was terrified. None of the textbooks mentioned her name. She searched for boyfriends to cover her terror. To play at the stories in all of the school books. She was in love with her female English teacher. Once she looked up lesbian in the medical dictionary. She worried about her hormones. When she was older she discovered the hidden world – the clubs and the pubs. She was still alone. She repeated to herself like a prayer.

BETH: It's just a phase; it will pass.

AISHA: But it didn't.

BETH *turns around. The lights brighten.*

BETH: No, thank God.

OPAL: Well I don't know if it's God you should be thanking!

OPAL *turns her back to them.*

BETH (*to* AISHA): How do you know all those things?

AISHA: I told you, I'm psychic.

BETH: You don't give away much.

AISHA: I'm not charity.

AISHA *tries to laugh and stops at the expression on* BETH's *face.*

BETH: Okay, I'll ask you straight . . .

AISHA (*interrupting her*): You never asked a straight question in your life.

BETH (*smiles*): How about this: do you fancy anybody?

AISHA (*nonchalantly*): Yeah.

BETH: Really? Who is it?

AISHA: You said it. I don't give much away.

BETH: Oh go on. I tell you things.

AISHA: What do you see in Opal? You two don't seem well suited.

OPAL *is indignant.*

BETH: Oh. We are.

AISHA: You want to know if 'it's' a man or a woman, don't you?

BETH: Yes.

AISHA: Guess.

BETH: A woman.

AISHA: Nah. I told you. It's not for me. Too risky.

BETH: Oh come off it, Aisha, you've always taken risks. Look at you being a carpenter. Opal? Have you heard this before?

OPAL *turns around and listens, unimpressed.*

When she was eleven she sat on one of her mum's new chipboard shelves and broke it.

AISHA (*to* OPAL): I was a bit of a podge then.

BETH: She felt so bad 'cos her mum didn't have an awful lot of money. She tried to fix it with superglue. She wished she could make them herself – fine pine shelves. Strong. Unbreakable. She looked at the table that wobbled on its shaky leg; she thought about making a cosy home for the gramophone. She decided then she was going to be somebody. Somebody who made things from wood. She started sketching distinguished desks, tremendous tables . . . Her imagination had a little set-back when her father came home and saw the superglued shelf. He wasn't

impressed was he when she told him –
'Never mind. One day I'm gonna be a
carpenter.'

OPAL *laughs.*

AISHA: Like I said, it's too risky.

AISHA *goes to the chest. The lights
soften.* YOMI *and* AISHA *take masks
from the chest and put them on.*

OPAL: Did you mean it when you said
we are suited?

BETH: Yes.

OPAL: Why?

BETH: You make me feel I can be myself
and . . .

OPAL (*interrupting her*): How long do
you think we'll last?

BETH: How do I know? I don't like
speculating.

OPAL: I'm scared of losing you. I can't
imagine my life without you now.

BETH: Opal, you're a real drama queen
sometimes. You were living before you
met me and you'll keep living if we
split.

OPAL (*hurt*): You must know what I
mean. I want to imagine growing old
with you.

BETH (*incredulous*): Old?

OPAL: Well if you're not there, who will
be? You're the only family I have,
Beth, the only one I can call home.
That's what freaks me out – what
happens when you go?

BETH: Why are we having this
conversation? I'm not going anywhere.
Do you see me heading for the door?
But I can't promise any forevers either.
I don't believe in always. Always is a
lie like till death do us part. Look at the
divorce rates amongst the straights.

OPAL: I'm not talking of marriage.

BETH: You are, Opal. (*Pause.*) Look
should we ever split up, and we might,
we'll leave each other stronger than we
were when we first met. Strong enough
to continue, Opal. Our love is filling me
up today. Tomorrow is something I
can't plan. Anyhow, I'm not the only
woman in the world, you know.

OPAL: Yes you are. Oh Beth. I love you

so much it's frightening. I don't trust
happiness. Why can't I say always?

BETH (*impatiently*): Because there is
nothing worse than shattered promises.
I love you too. I don't want to hurt
you.

OPAL: I understand. Promises used to
hurt so much – the foster parents that
never arrived. I used to feel so
unwanted. That's what terrifies me. I
feel wanted by you.

BETH: You are, honey. You're a wanted
woman.

*They start to dance close. The lights
go dim. As* AISHA *and* YOMI
*approach wearing masks and walking
like robots, the lights flash madly. The*
MUSICIANS *play intense, frightening
music.* AISHA *and* YOMI *break up
the dance; their movements are violent
but stylised.*

YOMI: Wanted for murder! For killing off
the race. God says it isn't natural. God
says it isn't natural. AIDS is God's
vengeance on the men. On the men.
Punishment for their sins. Their sins.
Man and woman. Adam and Eve.
That's the way it was meant to be.
Meant to be.

AISHA: It is sick. But it can be treated.
There is hope for them yet. Psychiatrists
are God's disciples. Aversion therapy.
Special diets. Electric shocks. A screw.
A screw.

YOMI: What do they do what do they do
these les-bi-ans? It is easy to imagine
what men do – but women, women.
The thought turns the national stomach,
stomach.

The robots walk off.

BETH: Is that your nightmare?

OPAL: Some of it.

OPAL *walks to the front of the stage.*
BETH *goes to the other side at the
back, so that she is diagonally
opposite.* AISHA *and* YOMI *return.
During* OPAL *and* BETH's *poems,*
AISHA *and* YOMI *match the words
with symbolic movement.*

OPAL: If I could tear it up
this fear that wears no soft gloves
could just banish all the *what ifs*
and twenty years from now

where will I be – how do dykes grow
    old?
I have this picture of Beth and I
loving all the finds
maturing like good wine
love keeping us warm
whenever I see it
love stretched over years
with plenty left to spread
I butcher the picture with my carving
    knife
and she is suddenly dead
I am at her funeral
and no one there knows what we meant
    to each other
and all her remaining relatives wonder –
who is the sobbing woman in the dark
    coat
at the back with a pew to herself?

The picture makes me want to say now
and for ever my name
tell them all where my loving lies
allowing them no weapon
for there is no bullet-proof protection
for the likes of us
and even though I have no family
I still turn my insides out
when I imagine what they would say
the old school friends, the old home
    friends
the nurses the doctors and all the
    anonymous
who should mean
Nothing
but might carry a knife
might follow me home
might write graffiti on my wall.

I want to banish it all
the dread that keeps all hours
and let me live my life
and let me live my love
and let me love my life.

Spotlight on BETH *who smiles
at* OPAL.

BETH: Yesterday the sky was white bright
    white
I couldn't see anything not even outlines
then, without warning, splashes of black
    and red
fire flies in the sky
inside me was a glow-worm glowing
the sky darkened to grey.

I never expected to be anything other
than alone – I am a wishing well
somewhere at the very bottom
I echo when touched

but I am hollow and it's a long way
    down

her need sucks like mosquitoes
my need is camouflaged
I am all green and brown
inside my leaves laugh and whisper:
you call yourself a risker?

Then I see another picture
we lie close talking tongues
she is under my skin
we are each other's dream
she and her opalescent eyes
me and my fire flies
we are dawn and dusk together

she is the first woman
to see all of me
and keep holding, holding.

BETH *and* OPAL *dance towards each
other and twirl each other around.
They join in* AISHA *and* YOMI's
*dance. The four dance together in a
dance of conflict and happiness. Wild
carefree music accompanies them.
Suddenly they separate.* YOMI *dances
to the front of the stage and sits down,
she tucks her imaginary child into bed.*
AISHA *and* BETH *and* OPAL
continue dancing through YOMI's
story. The lights soften.

YOMI (*to her child*): My mother told me,
    and her grandmother told her, that old
    Yomi was born with her tongue missing.
    People had never heard of such a thing.
    At first they were terrified, thinking that
    someone had done something wrong
    and this was the revenge. They spurned
    her: if it wasn't their fault, she must
    have brought it on herself.
        But. When as a child old Yomi
    started to draw and paint, people
    suddenly realised they were mistaken.
    She had a gift. They saw themselves in
    her pictures. They saw their grand-
    parents; they saw people they had not
    yet met. They saw people she could
    never have seen. She had powers. She
    was special.

YOMI *closes the imaginary door
quietly and walks to the edge of the
stage. She talks confidentially to the
audience.*

When I gave birth to Fabayo, I had the
most incredible experience. My waters
broke and she just slid out without any
problems. But, she never cried when

they spanked her. She didn't talk till she was three. I thought old Yomi was trying to pass something down and not quite making it! The other day I came home and Fabayo was drawing a picture of someone who in a funny way looks like Beth! That was what reminded me of the woman my mother called me after.

Lights go down and then up again. YOMI motions to the others who begin to walk around the stage in different directions frantically. They repeat.

ALL: I really hope it's going to be all right.

OPAL and YOMI open the chest. YOMI gives AISHA a loose black shirt. OPAL gives BETH some colourful wraps. OPAL takes out a red belt and ties it round herself. YOMI takes out a yellow skirt and puts it on. AISHA and BETH dress opposite each other to music in a stylised fashion; they are laughing nervously. YOMI and OPAL put some lipstick on each other. They separate. AISHA starts to move the chairs to the middle of the stage. YOMI and OPAL sit down on the chest, watching her. BETH walks round the stage, carrying an imaginary bottle of wine. She stops and presses an imaginary bell. (The MUSICIANS do the ding-dong!) AISHA opens the door.

BETH: Hello, Aisha. I'm a bit early.

AISHA: That's all right – you can help me set things up.

BETH gives AISHA the bottle of wine. They move the chairs.

AISHA: Thanks. Where's Opal, then?

BETH: She's coming along a bit later. She's still at the hospital.

AISHA: Oh good. For a minute, I thought she wasn't coming. Yomi should be here in a bit.

BETH: How is she?

AISHA: All right. (*Pause.*) Listen, Beth, I was going to ask you if you could tone it about the lesbian bit, 'cos Yomi doesn't know and . . .

BETH (*interrupting her*): Why didn't you tell her then?

AISHA: Well I didn't think that . . .

BETH: What?

AISHA: That you'd want me to.

BETH: Oh come off it, Aisha, since when have I kept it a secret?

AISHA: You look nice.

BETH: Thanks. Oh, I don't know; sometimes I just get really fed up with having to hide it from certain people in order to get on with them. I mean if they can't deal with it, it's their problem, not . . .

YOMI walks to the 'door'. She pushes the bell.

AISHA: That'll be Yomi, probably.

YOMI: Hello, Aisha.

AISHA: Yomi! How are you doing?

YOMI: Not bad, not bad at all.

They walk to BETH. YOMI eyes BETH's wrap with suspicion. BETH is upset. She lights a cigarette.

BETH: Hi Yomi, how are you?

YOMI: Well, thanks, and you?

BETH: Knackered. Too much work, you know.

AISHA: I've just got some bits to attend to, won't be long.

AISHA walks to the other end of the stage and stands still watching them.

YOMI: I like your wraps. Where are they from?

BETH: This friend of mine brought them from Nairobi. She went to the international women's conference there a few summers ago.

YOMI: Oh. (*Shouts.*) Aisha? Do you need a hand?

AISHA: No, I'm all right.

OPAL walks to the 'door' and pushes the bell.

BETH: Shall I get it?

AISHA: Go ahead.

BETH lets OPAL in. They kiss.

OPAL: Hello everybody.

AISHA walks back carrying 'food'.

AISHA: Hiya Opal, how's things?

OPAL: Oh all right.

YOMI: Fabayo's been asking when you're going to come and see us, ever since we bumped into you that day.

OPAL: Soon as I get an invite.

AISHA: Are you all ready to eat then?

BETH: Sure.

They concentrate on the 'food'.

BETH: A friend of mine is getting married tomorrow.

AISHA is surprised.

OPAL: Oh, who is that?

BETH: You don't know her.

YOMI: Are you going to the wedding?

BETH: Have to, really.

YOMI: You don't sound too enthusiastic.

BETH (*to* AISHA): Well, I really don't want to go on my own, and I couldn't take Opal with me. She's an old school friend. My mum knows her mum. My mum will be there too. I haven't seen her for a while. That'll be nice.

AISHA (*uncomfortable*): So . . . what have you been up to, Opal?

OPAL: Just work, work and more work. It seems to take up the whole of my life. I had a day of it today.

AISHA: Why, what happened?

OPAL: Well, I was telling one of my patients that it was curry for lunch and she said, 'It's not us that like that, but you coloured!' I didn't know what to say, so I just told her that I didn't like the word coloured, and she asked me what I'd call myself then. I told her black. She laughed and said, 'But you're a half-caste.'

BETH: Shit.

AISHA: What a cheek.

YOMI: What's wrong with half-caste.

AISHA: Come off it, Yomi!

YOMI (*angry*): Well. Tell me then! I've said it all of my life.

BETH: It's derogatory – it's just like all those other horrible descriptions: half-breed, mulatto, the lot. It really gets to me when people insist on saying that I'm half and half.

YOMI: But it's true, isn't it?

BETH: What do you mean?

YOMI: Well, you are half and half; you can't just pretend that you don't have a white parent. You can't say that you're not half white even if you don't . . .

BETH (*interrupting her*): Half white!

YOMI: Well, are you denying that your mother is white?

BETH: Of course not. That's not the point, is it? I mean . . .

YOMI: What is the point, then? You like theories, don't you? Theories aren't life.

AISHA: Yomi, what are you saying?

YOMI: I'm saying that Beth can't change what she is with theories.

BETH: Look, when I walk down the street and some NF thug wants to beat me up – what does he see, white or black? Is that a theory too?

YOMI: He won't want to beat you up as much as he'd want to beat me up.

BETH: Nonsense.

AISHA: This is getting too ridiculous for words. Competing to see who the NF wants to beat up the most! Honestly.

YOMI: You know, I still think there's some truth in that saying: if you're white, you're all right, if you're brown stick around, but if . . .

BETH (*interrupting her*): Why are you so suspicious of light-skinned women, Yomi?

YOMI: What? I'm not suspicious. Actually, if anything, I feel sorry for them. I don't envy the dilemma. I've always felt sorry for children of mixed marriages.

BETH: Thanks. I don't feel sorry for myself. I know where I belong.

YOMI: Good for you. Where is that?

AISHA: Yomi! You're just focusing on colour. Beth's talking about using the word black as a political statement.

YOMI: Exactly – a theory.

AISHA: You don't understand.

YOMI: Don't tell me I don't understand.

AISHA: You should never put anybody in the position of having to justify why they call themselves black. It pisses me off when Afro-Caribbean women tell me I have no right . . .

YOMI: I wasn't talking about that. Look, all I was trying to say (*To* BETH.) is that you needn't be ashamed of being half-caste. I mean, it's not as if you are illegitimate, is it?

OPAL: Meaning, I have got something to be ashamed of.

YOMI: Oops. Sorry. No. No, I don't think that at all. It's just that some people do. They're daft though. What was I saying, oh yes, Beth, don't try and cover up the fact that your blood is mixed, it's nothing to be . . .

AISHA: You still haven't got it, Yomi.

BETH: I am not denying my mother. I choose to call myself black. All this pure blood stuff is really dangerous.

YOMI: Really! Is this another theory? I came to eat food, not ideas.

AISHA: Can we talk about something else?

BETH: No.

OPAL: Let's forget it. God, I didn't realise what I was starting. Let me see, what else happened in my day . . .

BETH: Very funny.

OPAL: Well, Beth. I just think people ought to be able to say what they think without being afraid of someone jumping down your throat.

YOMI: Look I'm sorry if I've caused offence, it really wasn't intentional.

OPAL: That's okay. This food is delicious, Aisha. You've done a great job.

They concentrate on the food.

BETH: You were talking in your sleep last night, Opal.

YOMI *is shocked,* AISHA *is embarrassed.* OPAL *is terrified.*

OPAL: Was I?

AISHA (*quickly*): I've always wondered if I ever talk in my sleep. Nobody's ever told me, I suppose that's because . . .

BETH (*interrupting her*): It was funny. I kept wondering what you were dreaming. You just repeated, 'I'll do it, that's all right.'

YOMI *gets up.*

YOMI: Excuse me. I have to go to the bathroom.

YOMI *walks off and stands watching them.*

AISHA: What are you up to, Beth?

BETH: What do you mean?

AISHA: Oh come on. Look, I will not have my house used like this as some sort of fighting ring.

BETH: Tell that to your friend.

AISHA: This is wonderful this is.

OPAL: I think that was below the belt, Beth.

BETH: I have this strange feeling that I'm being ganged up upon. Must be another one of my theories.

AISHA: Beth!

YOMI *walks back to them.*

YOMI: Beth, I was thinking, you make things difficult for yourself, love. Life would be a lot easier if you didn't . . .

BETH: Tell me more!

YOMI: Well if you didn't go at everything with a hammer and chisel.

BETH: You're getting mixed up. Aisha's the carpenter.

YOMI: Every time I've met you, you've gone on the offensive about one thing or the other. Last time it was men. In fact you often go on about men. Why pay them all that attention, if you think they're so . . .

BETH: Rubbish! I hardly ever talk about men. I'm not interested . . .

YOMI: Well, that in itself . . .

OPAL: I think what Beth means . . .

BETH: I can talk for myself thank you, Opal.

AISHA: This is great, isn't it? I must have been mad to think we could all get on together. I invite you . . .

BETH: Wait a minute, Aisha. Yomi has just implied that . . .

OPAL: Forget it, Beth. Why are you getting so upset?

BETH: Well if you don't know that . . .

YOMI: I didn't imply anything. I only said that you are always on the offensive.

BETH: Have you ever thought about who puts me there? I just don't like pretence, that's all.

OPAL: Look, Beth, we have all come round to Aisha's place. She has cooked us a lovely meal. We only wanted to have a good time.

BETH: Good time!

YOMI: There is no need to be contemptuous about having a good time. There are enough bad times without cooking them up deliberately.

BETH: You must be the No. 1 chef then. It's not me that's made all this happen. You've been trying to wind me up all evening. I don't know what your problem is.

YOMI: Go on. Invent a theory. Honestly! You don't know how to relax, do you? It's a pity.

BETH: Look, if you want to come out with those things – go ahead, but don't expect me not to react to them. I can't live like that. (*To* OPAL.) You see, this is what I mean; it's not easy being . . .

AISHA (*interrupting her*): None of us have it easy, Beth. We all know that.

BETH (*close to tears*): I'm sorry, Aisha. I have to go. I can't take any more of this. I am not made of metal.

YOMI: Nobody said you were. Oh dear. Well, I'll be off too, Aisha. The food was wonderful, but . . .

AISHA: Great. Off you all go. Leave me the dishes and this horrible air. Oh I really wish I hadn't bothered.

OPAL (*goes over to* AISHA *and hugs her*): Oh Aisha, it's not your fault. We have to have arguments sometimes. Maybe they're even good for us.

AISHA: Oh yeah? Well you can count me out of the next one. I'd rather do something positively bad for me.

The lights go down and up again.
They all change mood suddenly.

AISHA: Well that bit is over. It was too near the bone.

BETH *goes to the* MUSICIANS *and*
gets percussion instruments from them.
She hands one to each woman. The
music starts. They all sing.

ALL: Yesterday was so strange a day
we each had to go our separate way
we believed the mirror held only one
    face
and it seemed like the world was empty
    of others.
Finding each other we have to find a
    place to say
those words we need to utter out loud
those words we need to hear
because there is nothing like fear.
Alone in it all – the black solo
searching for it in the rain
we were looking for
that meeting place
and we needed it bad
show us we are not the only ones
show us we are not the only ones.

Yesterday was so strange a day
it was not so easy as we thought it
    would be
we have to find that meeting place
or separate or separate again
and it will seem like the world is empty
    of others
and it will seem like the world is empty
    of others.

ACT TWO

The stage is the same as before. The two chairs and the stools make a bed in the middle. The lights are dim. There is a vague threatening music playing in the background. OPAL stands at one end of the stage peering into her imaginary mirror (the audience). BETH lies on the bed. AISHA and YOMI stand watching everything, next to the MUSICIANS. OPAL is wearing a long white T-shirt over her all-in-one-suit.

OPAL: It's you again. I might have known you wouldn't be gone for long. So what do you want me to do, welcome you back? I had a good break without you. Didn't miss seeing your ugly features one bit. Nor those funny eyes. The opals. Some precious stone you are. I could die and no one would notice. Beth would, I suppose. I'm not sure.

BETH (*looking through an imaginary photo album*): Here they all are; all different bits of past. All the various Beths. Here I am at six. A little black girl amongst the little white girls wearing bobbles in my hair, as if that would make me the same. I could never grow a ponytail. Opal reminds me. She reminds me of so much.

OPAL: I'll admit it. I was stupid to think I'm all right just 'cos some crazy black queer tells me so. Is that it? Why do I do this to myself? Maybe I am crazy after all. Maybe they should have just moved me from one institution to another. That's what you think, isn't it? It's strange, even although Beth is next door, I feel as if I have this house all to myself. Me and my ghosts. *You will always be alone.*

BETH: Someday I'd like to be able to be all of myself to all of those close to me. To have my mother love my lover. Sometimes I feel such a sham. When I was eighteen I rushed out and bought the black records that had never sat on my shelves, the blues, funk, jazz and soul I'd been missing. I bought books too. It was a whole new world. James Baldwin. Toni Morrison. C.L.R. James. I was excited. I dumped Dostoevsky, Dire Straits and Simon and Garfunkel. I pretended I'd never sang Joni Mitchell's 'Blue-oo-oo-oo-oo-oo-oo' to myself in the mirror.

OPAL: What would they say if they all knew? Opal, sweet friendly Opal is a pervert! What does a pervert look like? Do you know, can you tell at a glance walking down the street? When I first met Beth I was swimming in purple oceans, dancing on dangerous waters. I could let time go. I could let you go. Now you've come back, my boomerang reflection. You will always return, won't you. *Of course. Depend upon it.*

Yes. Smiling Opal is a mess. That's what you want to hear, isn't it? Beth is wrong. You were right all along. I was a fool to think any different. *Dry your nose will you? It's running. Your eyes look pathetic.* I don't want to know. Fuck you. I don't want to know.

The lights go down and up. They are flickering and flashing. AISHA and YOMI take cymbals from the MUSICIANS and play them to OPAL's song. BETH is sleeping. The music starts. It is soft and scary.

OPAL (*sings*): And I am waiting for discovery to come
one night that will have no tomorrow
one day that will come with no dawn
and fear hangs up doubts
a knowledge that sometime
would come this dusk –
soft and silent soft and silent

The lights go down. OPAL is rushing around the stage. She combs her hair and puts on a turquoise beret. YOMI gives her cymbal back to the MUSICIANS. She approaches OPAL.

OPAL: Yomi!

YOMI: Can't stop now. Got to rush.

BETH gets out of the bed slowly. AISHA walks towards BETH clanging the cymbal in a humorous manner. YOMI walks to the other end of the stage. AISHA passes BETH touching her lightly and then walks to the front of the stage. They form a triangle. OPAL is caught inside it.

YOMI: Hiya Opal.

She waves. OPAL rushes to YOMI.

Come here, darling.

OPAL stands in front of YOMI who looks right through her.

AISHA (*laughing*): Fool.

OPAL: Why are you laughing at me? Stop mocking me.

YOMI (*to* BETH): Tut. She has such a large ego, doesn't she? Thinks we can't laugh unless it's about her.

AISHA: Well, it's self-indulgence, isn't it?

OPAL: What are you all talking about?

BETH: Oh come on, Opal, you know. No good pretending now.

OPAL: *Beth*! Beth! Don't do this to me.

YOMI: Shit. She needs attention. Her adam's apple's jumping.

AISHA: Lost her rag.

The lights flash more, the music intensifies. BETH *runs to the bed and lies down on it.*

BETH: Nurse! Nurse! Nurse!

OPAL (*switches moods*): Yes. Yes Beth. I'll be with you in a minute.

BETH: Nurse!

OPAL: Coming. (*Going up to her.*) Okay. What's the problem? I get the feeling you like to keep me on my feet, Beth.

BETH (*whispers*): I know what you do on your back.

OPAL (*shocked*): Pardon?

BETH: I said I've got a sore back.

OPAL (*relieved*): Oh.

BETH (*mocking*): Oh you say Oh-*oh-oh-oh*.

OPAL (*takes her temperature*): You're very hot.

BETH (*whispers*): Not as hot as you.

OPAL: Pardon?

BETH: Get your hands off me.

OPAL: What did you say?

BETH: My hands hurt me.

OPAL *takes her pulse.* BETH *shoves* OPAL's *hands up her nightdress.*

Why don't you feel here. That's what you want.

OPAL *pulls her hand out, shocked.*

OPAL: I'm going to get . . .

BETH (*shouts*): Help, *help, help*.

YOMI *rushes up.*

YOMI: Did she touch you?

BETH (*smiling*): Yes.

YOMI: Oh dear. Doctor.

OPAL: Wait a minute. It's *her*. She's practically delirious. Feel her temperature.

YOMI: Now, now. We've had quite enough feeling for the one evening, Nurse Black.

AISHA *goes up to* OPAL, *clanging her cymbal. She leads* OPAL *to the back of the stage, gently.*

AISHA (*whispers*): It's all over now. It's better this way.

OPAL (*screams*): *I'm a good nurse.*

AISHA *and* YOMI *force* OPAL *to stand on the chest.* BETH *gets out of the bed. The music deepens.* OPAL *stands in a crucifixion position.* AISHA, YOMI *and* BETH *fire these questions like bullets.*

YOMI: Have you ever wanted to be a man?

OPAL: No.

YOMI: Were you ever raped?

OPAL: No.

BETH: Is it because you are too ugly to get a man?

OPAL (*turns around and stares at* BETH): *Beth Beth Beth.*

Lights down. Music stops abruptly. BETH *and* OPAL *lie on the chairs together.* AISHA *and* YOMI *sit down on the chest and watch them.* BETH *shakes* OPAL. *Lights up.*

BETH: You have to face it, Opal.

OPAL: Face my face, face my face.

BETH: Whatever it is you're afraid of. Stop running.

OPAL: My face is up like a big balloon. My eyes are swimming pools. My nose is an ape's nose. My lips are rubber. My face is dark and smooth. My cheeks are high and mellow. My eyes are deep and knowing. My nose sniffs new scents. My lips are soft and gentle. Which is me?

BETH: Both.

OPAL: I'm afraid I'll lose face.

BETH: With who?

OPAL: You, Yomi, lose face with myself. I have a string of boyfriends. I liked the feeling of a penis inside me!

BETH: So?

OPAL: So does that mean I'm not a real lesbian?

BETH: No of course it doesn't mean that.

OPAL: I can't take myself seriously. I've gone through my life taking on new things. Now all of a sudden I'm a black lesbian? What is that? It's a joke.

BETH (*furious*): It is not a joke.

OPAL: You make me sick. You go about all self-righteous, pretending you know the answers. I've seen into your dreams. They are not clean.

BETH: What rubbish are you talking? I think you need some sleep.

OPAL: You mean you need some sleep. I'm getting too much for you now. Why don't you just get rid of me then?

BETH: Oh Opal! Please.

BETH (*mimicking*): Opal! Please.

BETH: Stop it.

OPAL: Why?

BETH: You know why. You're just being destructive. I don't want to get into it.

OPAL: Oh nice choice. That's your choice. I wish I had the fucking choice.

BETH: You do.

OPAL: See! There you go again. Self-righteous. You think you know everything about me. Well you don't know fuck all.

BETH: Believe that if it makes it easier.

OPAL: Don't patronise me.

BETH: I can't say anything right can I? (*Softly.*) Tell me, Opal, what did I do to you in your dream?

OPAL (*shocked*): So you do know me.

BETH: A little.

Lights down. BETH and OPAL hug each other. Lights up. OPAL goes to YOMI. AISHA goes to BETH. YOMI and OPAL are painting. AISHA is making a cabinet. BETH watches AISHA.

YOMI: I just keep noticing more and more bumps. I suppose I'm a perfectionist. Nobody will notice but me.

OPAL *is very nervous. She can't relax. She is building up to talking.*

Fabayo wanted to help us today, but she's with her father. Just as well. (*Laughs.*) She'd have made a proper mess. Well, children need to see their father, don't they? I mean; it's not natural and I don't want to be the one . . .

OPAL: Yomi, do you think it's unnatural to be . . .

YOMI *looks at her strangely, waiting.*

Well, to have no father whatsoever?

YOMI: Oh dear. Have I put my foot in it again?

OPAL: No. No. Don't be silly. I just meant . . .

YOMI: Thank goodness for that. At least you're not as touchy as your friend.

OPAL (*ignoring that*): No I just meant if you were to choose to bring up a child on your own . . .

YOMI: Well if you're thinking about having kids, I tend to think, go ahead, why not, as long as it's loved . . .

OPAL: No I'm not. Beth wants kids though.

YOMI: Really? Has she got a boyfriend, then? Oh, I suppose it's none of my business.

OPAL: No she hasn't. Actually that's what I was wanting to talk to you about.

YOMI *is very wary. She doesn't want to hear what OPAL has to say. Whilst BETH and AISHA talk, OPAL and YOMI continue to paint, furious and concentrated.*

AISHA: Look, Beth, it's no good. We have to talk about it. I'm sorry, right, if you felt let down, but Yomi matters to me and I know some of her ideas are crap but she's been a good mate to me . . .

BETH: Aisha, you don't have to justify it all. I understand. I just wished you'd told me she was so homophobic.

AISHA: Homophobic. Listen to yourself.

Yomi probably thinks that means queer. Anyhow she doesn't even know, so . . .

BETH: Oh she knows all right.

AISHA: I'm just pissed off with the lot of you. That's all.

BETH: Why?

AISHA: You don't know a lot, do you?

BETH: I don't want to assume.

AISHA: Opal's welcome to you.

BETH (*shocked*): What do you mean?

AISHA: Ah forget it.

AISHA *concentrates on the cabinet. She is furious.* BETH *is upset and doesn't understand what's going on.*

OPAL: I've been telling myself I want to tell you and then thinking I should forget it.

YOMI (*ignoring her*): So. How would Beth get this baby?

OPAL: A donor probably.

YOMI: You're not serious! Ugh. Syringes and sperm, who could ask more from life?

OPAL: Well how else?

YOMI: Oh dear, did nobody tell you?

OPAL: You are so sarcastic sometimes.

YOMI: Do you think so? Really? I don't mean to be.

OPAL: Do you know then? After all. Beth was right.

YOMI: Know what?

OPAL: About me and Beth.

YOMI: Oh that!

OPAL (*starts to smile*): And it's all right with you? It doesn't bother you?

YOMI: Have you ever thought of getting married?

OPAL: What?

YOMI: Marriage. You know, ding-dong, paper . . . confetti.

OPAL (*giggling*): To tell you it straight. When I was a kid I used to have these fantasies of me and my lovely middle-class white husband and our children. I even had names for my children – Pauline, Graham and Amanda. I could even picture the little concrete garage for our car. Pathetic, isn't it?

YOMI: No.

OPAL: It's a myth. A big candy-floss lie.

YOMI: Speak for yourself. There are some that are happily married.

OPAL: So. It really doesn't bother you?

YOMI: Do you want it to? No. I just think it's a waste, that's all. But you must know that. I can't imagine what on earth you can . . . but it takes all types. I suppose I should have guessed sooner about Beth. But you. If it hadn't been for all that the other night, I would have never guessed about you. Not in a month of Sundays. I didn't want to believe it. Not about you.

YOMI *is sad and then she brightens.*

Anyway, maybe it's just . . .

OPAL: A phase?

YOMI *is surprised.*

YOMI: Well, you don't know, do you, what might happen. Never say never, that's my motto.

OPAL (*angry*): So you'd never say never to having a relationship with a woman?

YOMI (*shocked*): That's different.

OPAL: Why?

YOMI: It just is.

OPAL: And you said you weren't bothered.

YOMI: I'm not. It doesn't stop me thinking it unnatural, I mean . . .

OPAL: I've heard enough.

YOMI: How do you expect me to react?

OPAL: I don't know. I hoped that knowing me . . . I'm not suddenly a different person, you know, Yomi.

YOMI: Yes you are to me. I'm sorry, but that's how it is. It's not my fault.

OPAL: I wish you could hear yourself. I really do.

YOMI: Look. Don't look at me like that! As if I'm the one that's saying something terrible to you. You're the lesbian.

OPAL: I've heard enough. I really wanted to be friends but I just can't . . .

YOMI: Neither could I. Too many things to think about. What about Fabayo?

OPAL: What do you mean what about Fabayo?

YOMI: Well.

OPAL (*angry and hurt*): Yomi! You don't mean what you're saying.

YOMI: Oh, so you read minds too?

OPAL: This is the waste.

OPAL *and* YOMI *continue to paint.*

BETH: Aisha, we can't throw it all away.

AISHA: There's not a lot to throw, is there?

BETH: Don't be like that.

AISHA: You've got a nerve, Beth.

BETH (*angry*): You've got none, Aisha. I'm not crawling any more. Give me . . .

AISHA: Yeah, yeah, when I'm ready and all that sensitive shit. Why don't you shout or something? Feminists don't shout?

BETH (*exasperated*): Aisha. I don't understand. What did I do?

AISHA: Open your eyes then!

BETH: If it's . . . (AISHA *has turned her back to her.*) Oh . . . never mind.

Lights down. All four women freeze. OPAL sits down on the chest and watches AISHA and YOMI. BETH sits and watches them from the other side of the stage.

(*To* AISHA:) That's one of the worst bits.

AISHA: Are you kidding? Mine's to come.

AISHA *walks towards* YOMI, *who is still painting.* YOMI *turns around, furious.*

YOMI: You knew all along, didn't you?

AISHA: Knew what?

YOMI: Don't play games, Aisha. I'm not in the mood.

AISHA: Neither am I. If you've got something to say, say it.

YOMI: You knew about those two.

AISHA *stares at* YOMI.

YOMI: Oh come on, Aisha. They're a couple of lezzies, aren't they?

AISHA: That's not a word I'd use.

YOMI: I've made a complete fool of myself!

AISHA: How come?

YOMI: You could have told me.

AISHA: I thought you'd find out in your own time. It wasn't for me to tell. Anyhow, what difference does it make?

YOMI: If it doesn't make any difference, why did you hide it?

AISHA: I didn't hide anything. You are the one who was hiding.

YOMI *stares at* AISHA.

AISHA: You picked it up, but you didn't want to believe it 'cos you liked Opal and so you just pretended to yourself that you hadn't seen what you saw.

YOMI: Nonsense, though I might have guessed about Beth. (*Pause.*) Anyhow they can't even keep lasting relationships with each other. I don't imagine Beth and Opal will be together long.

BETH *and* OPAL *pull faces at each other across the stage.*

AISHA: You and your husband lasted ages of course.

YOMI: At least we were in a natural relationship.

AISHA: Oh yeah?

YOMI: Yeah. If we were all meant to be like that, no one would exist, would they? . . .

AISHA (*interrupting her*): If you want to worry about generations, why don't you worry about the neutron bomb?

YOMI: She really wanted to shock me too. Well I wasn't giving her that. I wasn't handing it to her on a plate.

AISHA: Who are you talking about?

YOMI: I liked her too.

AISHA: Past tense? Yomi! I would have thought you could have done better than this.

YOMI: Why are you defending them so ardently? Don't tell me . . .

AISHA: What if I am?

YOMI: Don't, Aisha. I can't take jokes at the moment.

AISHA: Suit yourself.

YOMI (*bewildered*): You're not, are you?
I would definitely know if you were
one. (*Pause.*) Well. If you think you're
a lesbian, I'm really sorry.

AISHA: What are you sorry about?

YOMI: Aisha, stop messing around.

The lights go down. BETH *and* OPAL
*start to dance slowly matching each
other's movements like an echo. They
are still at opposite ends of the stage.*
AISHA *and* YOMI *look at each other
during their poems as if they are still
continuing their conversation.*

AISHA: It is just the wondering
the small frail maybe
the pushing away
before it can settle –
I am like they are
terrified of plunging
into that unknown country
the landscapes with no familiar trees
    or flowers
the vastness of the moors
the never endingness of the earth rolling
fear can stop a dream beginning
and wondering is wandering in the dark
stranger's voice echoing
yearning for that other woman
to hold me close –
could I sink into her depth?

BETH *and* OPAL's *dance becomes
more brittle. They jar with their bodies.
The light goes blue.*

YOMI: I just pictured it blue
not the blue of the sea
but the blue of the blues
and bruises, how could anyone
be happy that way
touching the very core of
anti creation; how could
someone love unnatural
like the last rays of sunshine
how could she feel hot for she
and want the heat on her back
like the pounding midday sun
opening the pores for the sweat to run

The lights soften. AISHA *takes a step
forward.*

AISHA: It is the terror of beginnings
where the end cannot be envisaged
malicious words sitting on the edge
of my tongue, where *I want* is
    smothered,
the terror of endings.

And the family, the family
what would they say
and knowing anyway that I could say
    nothing
the emptiness of the unspoken years
how long could I live a lie?
how long would the air stifle me in that
    closet?
Yet the smell of an unwanted husband's
    breath
in the morning would make me
long for those uncertain moors.

The lights glare. BETH *and* OPAL
*dance facing outward, not looking at
each other. Their movements are hard.*

YOMI: And I pictured it ugly
like the ugliness of something
you don't want to look at
imagining one might accost me
in the Ladies' restroom
as soon as I heard lesbian
I saw ugly and blue
and lonely and not being able to get
THE REAL THING
and a tall angular looking woman
white with men's things on,
too much hair around the mouth
and always on the prowl
she was so lonely
would die lonely
never knowing any kind of love
because lesbian and love
could not come together
like man and woman

The lights soften. BETH *turns around
and starts to dance towards* OPAL
*who dances on the spot, with confident
steps.*

AISHA: And my landscape
is coloured in browns and reds:
she walks firm steps over it
I envy her
the way she's making history
whilst she walks, the implications of the
foot steps left behind
I follow them, sink into shapes
a wood pigeon calls at dawn
lights uncertainty creates morning
    shadows
I watch her go
that sturdy black woman walking
can just see her dark hair swing
I want to go with her.
I want to go with her.

The lights stay soft. OPAL *and* BETH
*start to dance closely together, happy.
They whirl and twirl each other*

around. YOMI *watches them. At the end of her poem, they freeze into an album photograph.*

YOMI: I pictured ugly and lonely
that was my only bit of sympathy
and I couldn't see anyone
or smiles and softness and need
like Beth and Opal
looking good together
dark eyes lit by the fire in her
dark eyes sparkling at the woman in her
dark eyes dancing
out the need of time
I looked at Beth and Opal
and I looked at my old pictures
I had to get out those albums
and go over the years.

The lights go down and up again.
OPAL approaches YOMI and takes
her hand. BETH *smiles at* AISHA.

OPAL: We are still going over the years.

AISHA: We are running out of time.

BETH (*to* YOMI): Are you going to?

YOMI: I don't want to run anymore.
I was remembering something my
mother told me. She said there were
these women she used to know in
Nigeria who lived with their husbands
but loved each other. She said, God it
surprised me so much, that it was a
pity they had to hide, a pity they
couldn't just live together out in the
open, if that's what they wanted.

AISHA (*looks at her watch*): This is the
one I remember the best. The first time
I heard Opal sing it, it made me cry.

OPAL: Don't cry this time, Aisha. Sing!

BETH *goes to the* MUSICIANS *and*
gets percussion instruments. She
distributes them.

AISHA (*to* OPAL): Are you ready?

OPAL: Are you?

AISHA: Yeah. All right.

AISHA *starts to play her instrument.*
They all start to dance. The others
harmonise as OPAL *sings.*

OPAL (*sings*): They had no one to name
me after
in so many different ways
so tell me what do you call her
a woman who loves another like her
what do you call her

where are her people
who are her ancestors
tell me what is her name
tell me what is her name

I want to find it all now
know our names know the others in
history
so many women have been lost at sea
so many of our stories have been swept
away
I want to find the woman
who in Dahomey 1900
loved another woman
tell me what did they call her
did they know her name
in Ashanti, do they know it in
Yoruba do they know it in patois
do they know it in Punjabi
do they know it in Arabic
do they know it in Hindi
do they know it in Cantonese
do they know it in English

do you think my mother is still living
and would she like to have a daughter
who is a lesbian, would she call my
name
tell me would she know my name?

The lights go down. They hand back
their instruments. AISHA *hugs* OPAL.

AISHA: You are brave. Do you think
you'll try and trace her?

OPAL: I might. Some day. I'm not in a
hurry anymore.

YOMI (*to* BETH): I'm sorry.

BETH: Don't say sorry.

YOMI: But I am.

BETH: Sorries are never going to get us
anywhere.

AISHA: Oh come on. They're a start.

BETH: They're a stop.

OPAL (*laughing*): We can't even agree
on sorry. (*To* BETH.) You have to
change too. Change isn't compromise.

BETH: Oh no?

OPAL (*firmly*): No.

BETH: What is it then?

OPAL *goes to the chest. She takes the*
mirror out.

OPAL: It is all this.

She gives YOMI *the mirror.*

Yesterday I looked in her and she said to me: it's not me that's changed – it's you. I liked myself!

YOMI (*defensively*): It doesn't happen overnight, you know. A lifetime under these eyes. Seeing the way I saw. You want to get me some new eyes? I banished so much from my sight. Sometimes that's bliss.

She looks critically at herself in the mirror.

(*To* BETH:) It's true, isn't it? I mean sometimes you don't want to look at yourself.

BETH: Or out. You know I used to pride myself in being so active politically. Maybe it was a secret alternative way of getting to Heaven. But so much of me was still hiding. At least some of my desires. And I locked the past that gave me no kudos away.

BETH *goes to the chest and takes out the album. She gives it to* AISHA, *who is surprised.*

AISHA: It's not the same.

BETH: I know. I'm not pretending it is.

AISHA (*angrily*): Pretence was always a murderer.

BETH: All I'm saying is, don't chop yourself into little bits. Be it all.

AISHA: How can I? It's luxury.

BETH: No, it's necessity. I know now, Aisha. I'm sorry I couldn't see for looking.

AISHA *is embarrassed.* YOMI *goes to the chest and takes the doll. She gives it to* BETH, *who is shocked.*

It's all come round.

YOMI: You've not come round.

BETH: Now it's a game.

YOMI: Oh no. It was never a game. It was serious. See this baby you want to have?

BETH (*defensively*): Yeah?

YOMI: Give this to her. Give her a name if you like. I could never give her to Fabayo.

BETH (*takes the doll appreciatively and laughs*): I've made up so much. This is all make-believe. Now I want it to be real. Stop acting, will you?

OPAL: We can't. We are real. Feel.

AISHA: Here we go again. Do you think by the next time we'll have stepped forward?

YOMI: Certainly.

AISHA *goes to the chest and takes the cushion out. She gives it to* OPAL.

AISHA: We're moving on. You can make your own tales of generations after generations. Invent yourself.

OPAL: That's what we're all doing, isn't it?

AISHA: I'm working at it. It's lonely sometimes.

BETH *takes* AISHA*'s hand.*

YOMI: That's funny. I remember you standing exactly there and saying those lines, and Beth . . .

OPAL (*laughing*): Yeah, yeah, yeah. Déjà vu vu vu. Okay, Aisha, it's down to you.

BETH: Wait a minute. You forgot the song.

OPAL: Oh yeah.

She motions to the MUSICIANS. *They start playing.*

ALL (*sing*): If we should die in the wilderness
let the child that finds us
know our name and story
know our name and story
let us never forget to remember
all our heres and theres
let a hot sun shine on our wishes
let the rain fall without our tears

and we will look for our landscapes
listening to the river running
knowing we are different from each other
but we still have something to share
scraping at the skies together
scraping at the skies together.

If we should die in the wilderness
let the child that finds us
know our names and stories
know our names and stories
we cannot afford to fall apart
we can create out of chaos
rubble and dust can build a dream for us

If we should die in the wilderness
let us go down singing our forbidden songs

for life
let us go down remembering
old Yomi could not talk but she could
    tell stories
old Yomi could not talk but she could
    tell stories.

*They all start to dance. The music
changes to the same tune as in the
beginning.*

ALL: Time changes light
  light changes time
  there we were with the dawn in the
    dark
  the dark in the dawn
  trying to find the words
  trying to find the words

These lines overlap.

AISHA: This is how we got to where we
  are. My name is Aisha, remember,
  I was called after my grandmother on
  my mother's side.

BETH: My name is Beth. I was called
  after my great-great-great-great
  grandmother on my father's side.

OPAL: My name is Opal. I was called
  after some old woman's earrings.

YOMI: My name is Yomi. I was called
  after old Yomi. Remember her?

*Lights down. They exit, leaving the
doll, the album, the cushion and the
mirror in the same position as they
were in the beginning. They re-enter.
BETH watches the audience. AISHA
opens the chest. OPAL and YOMI
stand and chat to each other about the
performance. Lights out.*

Chiaroscuro

In the spring of 1985 Theatre of Black Women asked me to write a short performance piece which would run for thirty minutes. Had they asked me to write a full length play that would run for three months I would have said no, simply because I wouldn't have thought it possible. Theatre of Black Women read my original draft, which I was then calling *The Meeting Place*, and asked me to expand it to an hour. I did so. This was then read at the Drill Hall as part of the Gay Sweatshop Times 10 Festival. It was, to my amazement, well received.

Theatre of Black Women then organised a four-week period of workshops around the script which were directed by Joan Ann Maynard. I fed the inspiration and the motivation from these workshops into a reworking of the play. *Chiaroscuro* would never have been the same without them. The workshops developed a plot, which the original draft did not have, and added flesh to my rather thin-boned characters. Yomi was particularly skinny! Through improvisations, games and background work, the four women in the play began to form with more solidity. I rewrote the script to include as much as possible from the workshops. It was this version of the play which was produced and toured for three months.

I realised when I saw the final production of the play that there were major problems with its structure and its style. The dialogue and the poetry were not sufficiently interwoven. There was an unhappy combination of realism and symbolism. Some of the dialogue was so naturalistic that the poetry jarred with it rather than complemented it. The end of the play just did not work. I decided then that if it was ever published I would need to go in for draft number three.

This time around I returned to my original idea, which placed more emphasis on the symbolic. I wanted to get away from some of the flat and heavy naturalism which sat uncomfortably in the production. I returned to the first idea that I'd had, whilst I was sitting in my parents' garden in Glasgow, for this play: that the four women had all met already and that the play would be an elaborate déjà vu. I brought back into the play the chest which was crucial in the first draft and which got lost in the production. The chest is an important symbol; it functions as the past and also as the chest in the human body. In order to breathe, these four women have to get things 'off their chest'. Everything that is important to them is contained in the chest.

This time around I also returned to the idea that time and the space were not important. What is important is what is happening and what has happened. I needed to find something that would make the play work on different levels, and that would connect to the main themes of the play. In the end, after much painful struggling and many displacement activities (my room has never been so tidy), the idea grew upon me that all of these four women had invented themselves and together they made up the play. This explains why they already knew each other. They all see the play, the journey, as part of a painful and enjoyable process that they have to go through, and which they've been through already.

In all of the drafts of this play I have been obsessed with naming. What do we call ourselves as lesbians and black women? How did we get our names? How do we assert our names? What are our past names? Each of the characters tells the story of her name. She is also searching for another name. She is in flux, reassessing her identity, travelling back into memory and forward into possibility. In order to change we have to examine who we say we are and how much of that has been imposed. The more these four characters perform this play the closer they get to who they are.

In all versions of *Chiaroscuro* my main interest has been communication. Can these four women communicate or not? What do they say with their silence? What don't they say with their words? I wanted to show how difficult communication is in a racist and homophobic society. As Ntozake Shange says 'oppression/makes us love one another badly/makes our breathing mangled'. (Ntozake Shange, *Three Pieces*, Penguin Plays).

I am committed to change, personal and political, and everything I write comes out of this commitment. Writing *Chiaroscuro* was a challenging and terrifying experience. Part of the terror is needing people to hear what it is you have to say and at the same time worrying that they are not listening.

I think I have said everything I can here, the rest is in the play, except to say that many writers influenced *Chiaroscuro*; Ntozake Shange in particular. I was reading *For Colored Girls* . . . before I began the play and was impressed by the way she made poetry work as theatre.

Jackie Kay
1987

List of plays performed by Theatre of Black Women

1982   *Tiger Teeth Clenched Not to Bite* by Bernardine Evaristo
       Hey Brown Girl by Patricia Hilaire
       Chameleon by Paulette Randall
       A triple-bill of one-woman shows.

1982   *Silhouette* by Patricia Hilaire and Bernardine Evaristo
       The play draws parallels between a Black woman who died in slavery 200
       years ago and a young mixed race Black woman of today.

1984/5 *Pyeyucca* by Bernardine Evaristo, with additional material by Patricia Hilaire
       A play about how a Black woman's self-image is conditioned by white society
       and about how she could break out of that imprisonment.

1986   *Chiaroscuro* by Jackie Kay

1987   *The Cripple* by Ruth Harris
       A one-woman show about the real-life story of a physically disabled Jamaican
       woman.

1987   *Miss Quashi and the Tiger's Tail* by Gabriela and Jean Pearce
       A play for children.

THE RUG OF IDENTITY

The Rug of Identity was first performed at the Oval House Theatre, London, by Hard Corps on 5 February 1986, with the following cast:

PRISON OFFICER	Heather Gilmore
JOANNA	Debby Klein
MONA	Sarah McNair
LAURIE	Cathy Kilcoyne
MRS PROCTOR	Karen Parker
SCOTTISH HOT-DOG SELLER	Heather Gilmore
FIRST MUGGER	Sarah McNair
SECOND MUGGER	Heather Gilmore
HARVEY	Himself

Directed by Jude Alderson
Designed by Amanda Wilson
Costumes by Catti Calthrop

Scene One

Death Row, 8.30 p.m.

PRISON OFFICER *sits at desk.*
Telephone, papers and pen on desk.
MONA *sits in her cell behind prison bars,
knitting a wreath; ribbons, scroll, radio at
her feet. Lights up on* PRISON OFFICER.

PRISON OFFICER (*plays telephone
ring*): Ring ring. Death Row, can I help
you? Yes, we do have a vacancy for a
hangman's assistant. Have you had any
experience in this type of work? Only
Birch and Castigation? Well, we've had
applications from Oxbridge grads so you
see the sort of competition you're up
against. Yes, being sexist and racist does
help. If you'd like to give me your name
and address I'll get a form out to you
tomorrow. B. Mayall. What does the B.
stand for? Belinda? Oh I'm sorry, we
don't take women, we don't really think
they're suitable for the job, do you?

JOANNA *enters behind* PRISON
OFFICER *carrying a letter and a
bunch of flowers. She is wearing a
green shimmering tie.*

PRISON OFFICER: Visiting hours are
over.

JOANNA: I have special permission to
visit my mother.

PRISON OFFICER: A relative of the
hangee are you? (*Takes letter from*
JOANNA.) Comes from the top, all
right, Cell 16. Better hurry she's due on
the scaffold at nine. I shall have to ask
you to remove your tie, Sir.

JOANNA: I am NOT a Sir!

PRISON OFFICER: Sorry, Madam.
Some of us are lost without a strip
search.

JOANNA: I hope it'll be returned to me
unadulterated. This garment is invested
with a meaning few women can
understand.

PRISON OFFICER (*dawn of
recognition*): Your mum's told me all
about you. She's very proud. (*They
move towards* MONA. PRISON
OFFICER *stops* JOANNA *from going
forward.*) Still, she may not recognise
you. Be prepared for anything.

They walk round MONA's *cell twice.*

*Sound effects, cries of torment, wailing.
Lights up on* MONA.

PRISON OFFICER (*opens imaginary
door with keys*): Creak.

Music from radio – 'The Archers'.
MONA *is knitting her wreath.*

PRISON OFFICER: Mona, there's
someone here to see you.

MONA: It'll be that young fellow who
measured my neck, probably come to
tell me they haven't got my size in
noose.

JOANNA: Mummy?

MONA: Darling! What a lovely surprise.
Have you come to see me swing? And
you've brought me flowers, how
comforting, they're so much nicer than
wreaths. Joanna, you're NOT crying,
are you? If you're going to blub they'll
have you removed. Isn't that right,
PO?

PRISON OFFICER: That is correct,
Madam. I'll pop back nearer the time.
(*Blows a kiss – exits.*)

JOANNA: Oh Mummy, Mummy,
Mummy, Mummy.

MONA: Your conversation is as dogmatic
as ever, I see.

JOANNA: It's the shock of seeing you
here.

MONA: Well Joanna, I'm just as
surprised to see you. I thought you
were going to hate me till your dying
day, not mine.

JOANNA: I'm here, aren't I? What does
that suggest to you?

MONA: That you're free and I'm not.

JOANNA: I couldn't bring myself to
come before.

MONA: To see your own mother.

JOANNA: To see a murderer.

MONA: Doesn't matter. I haven't wanted
to see anyone. I've been in love. (*Plays
with wreaths and ribbons.*)

JOANNA: In love?

MONA: With a Prison Officer.

JOANNA *thinks of Prison Officer.*

Mmm. I told her if she didn't lock me
in I'd be unfaithful to her.

JOANNA: Oh Mother, how could you?

MONA: I know, I have appalling taste, but at least I know she's not going to be unfaithful to me.

JOANNA: Don't you realise that you've enforced at least two stereotypes. One, that ugly women make the most faithful lovers and two, that prisons are a hot bed for lesbians.

MONA: I don't agree with that at all. Some prisons are notoriously frugal when it comes to giving out blankets. But I will tell you something about stereotypes. Not all women who carry handcuffs are into S and M.

JOANNA: Oh God!

MONA: Oh Joanna. You take things so seriously. Life is supposed to be fun. Let me see this GAY side of you that's reportedly always been suppressed.

JOANNA: I am NOT gay. I consider any sort of enjoyment of life as it is to be in the worst political taste.

MONA: Sometimes I think you chose to be a lesbian so you could be justifiably miserable for the rest of your life.

JOANNA: I didn't choose to be a lesbian. YOU pushed me into it.

MONA: Joanna, that is NOT true.

JOANNA: Well, even so. I'm not a lesbian, what you see is just a façade.

MONA: How do you know? Have you given it a chance?

JOANNA: Marilyn did a urine test on me.

MONA: And?

JOANNA: I turned red not pink. I can't show my face anywhere. I'm sure people at the Centre will know.

MONA: I've always steered clear of the Centre, they're terribly middle-of-the-road, and people who walk down the middle of the road get run over.

JOANNA: It's even worse when I'm with heteros. I feel like a consonant when I want to be a vowel.

MONA: But darling, we all make the same sounds in bed.

JOANNA: I can't understand it, Mummy. I had all the right contractions and swellings.

MONA: But not for Marilyn.

JOANNA: Our relationship was never consummated.

MONA: That is an improper use of the word 'relationship'. We are not related to HER.

JOANNA: Anyway. I've moved back to the house and I've given up on sex.

MONA: What? Joanna, just when are you going to grow up? Couldn't you have slept on a friend's floor like any other self-respecting homeless lover?

JOANNA: She was full up. Besides, that house is my home, my inheritance.

MONA: And do you want to inherit my loneliness too? Celibacy will exclude a lot of people from your life.

JOANNA: I'll never be alone. I'm an accomplished flirt. Aren't I?

MONA: Are you? Oh yes, you can play the field when you're young, there are always plenty of women willing to tease, but they all go back to procreation in the end, and where will that leave you?

JOANNA: Out in the fields leaping with the lambs I hope.

MONA: No it won't. You'll find yourself standing in a corner of one of those awful bars wishing you could . . . pop out of your body. You can't abstain for the rest of your life. You've got to take responsibility for your swellings and contractions like everyone else.

JOANNA: You've never had a contraction in your life . . . My father was a gentleman.

MONA: Your father was a lavatory seat. I conceived you in the Gents at Charing Cross.

JOANNA: But . . . you always said I was an A.I.D. Child.

MONA: The 'A' stands for Anonymously.

JOANNA: I have a father – a REAL father? A human being capable of making mistakes?

MONA: Darling, I wouldn't romanticise it too much if I were you.

JOANNA: Was it 'up' or 'down'? Perhaps I should be a boy.

MONA: I believe it was down at the time,

and the environment was as sticky as it should have been.

JOANNA: My father! I wonder if he's looking at a toilet seat now – thinking of me.

MONA: In that particular position I doubt if he's thinking of a woman.

JOANNA: Tell me all you know about him. Was he . . . (*Like an actress.*) good looking, like me? Mummy I've a right to know, especially now.

MONA: Well, it's a long time ago, of course, and the night was as foggy as my memory is now, but I remember the tiles gleamed bright in the pale moonlight, and somewhere a cistern flushed the sky with crimson. I was desperate . . .

JOANNA: I don't want to hear about you, I want to hear about HIM.

MONA (*curtly*): All I can remember is, as they came out he had a very red face.

JOANNA: Oooh! Like me.

MONA: I doubt if you'll find the key to yourself in the common ability to blush like a tomato. You might as well claim genetic affiliation with a sauce bottle. (*Sternly.*) What's past is past. It's your future you ought to be thinking of. I still regard you as my daughter, whatever feelings you may have for me, and I've made sure you won't ever be penniless as I was. (*Produces a document tied by red ribbon.*)

JOANNA (*cheers up*): You've left me the house.

MONA: I'm leaving you a great deal more than a house. You can't make much from that twiddle-twaddle you write . . .

JOANNA: I still sell. I may have no great literary talent but I am prolific. Your bedtime stories will last me a lifetime.

MONA: My bedtime stories? I don't think they're suitable for children.

JOANNA: I don't write for children any more. Haven't you read any of my books?

MONA: No sweetheart, I've had the business to run, and you know how critical I am.

JOANNA: You wouldn't have been, had you read them. I got all my ideas from you. I hardly changed a word.

MONA: Good God! You PRINTED those stories.

JOANNA: As 'thrillers' they're a knockout.

MONA: What was your last bestseller?

JOANNA (*unaware*): The Lollypop Lady . . . Once upon a time there was a Lollypop Lady who got pushed under a car . . . It's a wonder I didn't have nightmares.

MONA: I DID. I terrified myself.

JOANNA: And what about . . . The Water Babies. About the swimming instructor drowned in his bath. Who dunnit?

MONA: His wife, because he was sleeping with his pupils all under age. The wife, as I remember it, couldn't swim.

JOANNA: Actually some of them were terribly funny.

MONA: And fun to do.

JOANNA: What do you mean . . . 'fun to do'?

MONA: Fun! . . . amusing . . . stimulating . . . I ENJOY killing.

JOANNA: Mummy, you're getting fact and fiction mixed up. You've only murdered once.

MONA (*booms*): ONCE! Good gracious no! HUNDREDS of times . . . Child benefit wasn't very much in your day, and I got used to the extra pennies. I was also bloody good at it. It's the only thing I've ever done well.

JOANNA: Keep your voice down.

MONA: Oh, I SEE. Everybody else's mother can be a professional assassin, but not yours. I'm nothing to be ashamed of. You should be pleased for me. Not every woman finds fulfilment and riches so early in life.

JOANNA: Professional assassin . . . The Manet above the fireplace when everyone else had the reproduction print, the cheerful way you'd quote Lady Macbeth over the washing machine, the locked cellar where you told me you kept your contraceptives . . . I thought it was all part of a middle-class education. Oh God! Why didn't I see it before?

MONA: You were too busy looking for your clitoris, darling, and had I told you, you might have tried to take away the only pleasure I've ever had. And you wouldn't have understood, Joanna. You see, when you were little, men stopped taking notice of me, and that was very hard for a woman who's always been surrounded by them. And when men stop taking notice, women stop too. Suddenly nobody took any notice of me . . . Not even the Lollypop Lady.

She throws her documents on the floor in anger. JOANNA *winces.*

That one was for me. From then on I murdered for others who felt as I did. Not indiscriminately. Only for women . . . Women who were neglected and uncared for, bartered and betrayed . . . 'He doesn't need me anymore.' The number of times I've heard that, Joanna. AND they paid well. And only one of them regretted it. The woman who 'grassed' on me.

JOANNA: Then you could have named her. Why did you deny all knowledge of her in court?

MONA: I believe in a different kind of justice, Jo. We were partners in crime, rather like you lesbians and feminists.

JOANNA: But you murdered a woman, I don't see anything liberating in that.

MONA: A man, a woman, what's the difference? Their deaths sold your books. AND the story of my life and death will sell many more. Now I want the world to know what I did. (*Thumps the pile of papers.*)

JOANNA: You haven't gone and got yourself a biographer, have you?

MONA: I've got the best.

JOANNA: Norman Mailer?

MONA: She's standing right opposite me. Who better than my own daughter?

JOANNA: ME! Impossible. Don't you realise that would crack open my whole identity as a writer of fiction. My reputation, my whole existence would be pulled out from under my feet.

MONA: Darling, I must tell you, I still haven't decided about the house.

JOANNA: Well Mummy, you'd better, it's almost nine now.

MONA: So I've had an agreement drawn up with my lawyer whereby you will inherit all my property on the event of the book's publication, and NOT before. (*Picks up knitting needle, slashes wrist, dips point into blood.*) I'd like it signed in blood, please, reduces the risk of forgery.

JOANNA *hesitates.*

No book . . . No house.

JOANNA: How can you do this to me? I've never written anything without knowing the 'why', wheres and who dunnits'. I'll be stumbling in the dark.

MONA: I'm well aware of the limits to your imagination, I remember the trouble you had with tampax as a teenager. You'll find all the background information you require here. (*She picks up a portfolio.*) Gambell is the name of my last client. She has a bank account in Milton Keynes.

JOANNA: There must be at least . . . three Gambells in Milton Keynes. How on earth am I to recognise the right one?

MONA: She will be carrying about her person the second finger of a left hand, rolled in gold. The trick will be to trap her into revealing it.

JOANNA (*signing*): The second finger of a left hand. Oh God! None of this would be happening if I could have provided the police with a watertight alibi. I shall always blame myself for being in bed with Marilyn at the time.

MONA: It wasn't so incredible. Freud claims that there are always four persons involved in the sexual act.

JOANNA: You were all right, Mummy, it was the fourth I couldn't provide an alibi for.

JOANNA *finishes signing.* PRISON OFFICER *enters and opens door of cell.*

MONA: Time's up. Better go now, sweet. (*She gives her the portfolio, the document with ribbon that she has just signed.*) I'm putting my legacy in your hands. In a few minutes I shall be a human pendulum. Think . . . is that how you want to remember your mother?

JOANNA: God no! I shall have enough trouble altering my birth certificate as it is.

MONA: All my love, Jo. This will be a test of yours.

Lights close round her. PRISON OFFICER *and* JOANNA *walk twice round the cell, moans, groans and wailings in the background. The* PRISON OFFICER *goes back to her desk.*

JOANNA: I should like to have my mother sectioned as quickly as possible, it was her last wish.

PRISON OFFICER: Your mother has never communicated such a desire to me.

JOANNA: She was afraid it might influence your orgasm.

PRISON OFFICER: That's how I'll remember her. Unselfish to the point of frigidity.

JOANNA: So you admit that you abused your position of power.

PRISON OFFICER: I'll admit I had my eye on her silk ribbons, but intimacy would have taken place for less. I was finally seduced by her 'Dance of the Wreaths', although I'm not a scholar I read something into it.

JOANNA: And you conclude that she was insane and not responsible for her actions.

PRISON OFFICER: If need be, Madam.

JOANNA: Good!

She shreds document with ribbon.

PRISON OFFICER: Do you wish to be present at the hanging?

JOANNA: No.

The ribbon drops on floor, later to be worn around MONA's *neck in Scene 4.*

PRISON OFFICER: Then if you'd care to sign for your mother's personal effects.

JOANNA: Certainly. (*Signs paper.*)

PRISON OFFICER: If there's any chance that the ribbons . . .?

JOANNA: Of course. (*She gives her the ribbon from the document.*)

PRISON OFFICER: And if there should be a miraculous resurrection. How shall we contact you?

JOANNA: I shall be at home. No. I shall be at the Chaps at Charing Cross. The place where they won't let you in unless you're accompanied by a man.

PRISON OFFICER: I'm sure your Lady Mother would approve. This way, Madam.

Exit back right. Lights out.

Cast change scene to the music 'A Woman's Touch' sung by Doris Day.

Scene Two

LAURIE's *flat, close to Charing Cross.*

Same day, 9.45 p.m. Living room, with sofa, small table with telephone on it, chair near table, tailor's dummies, screen on the left at the back. Front door is just a door frame back right. Two bedrooms offstage left. LAURIE's *and spare room. Kitchen also offstage back left. Bathroom offstage, wherever. A toilet pedestal is hidden behind the sofa for the next scene change.*
  It has been raining outside.
  Music of 'A Woman's Touch', while LAURIE *is arranging material on male dummy.* MRS PROCTOR *arrives on stage dragging a crocodileskin suitcase and a trunk. She stops before the doorframe and plays the door bell.*

MRS PROCTOR (*curt and impatient*): Ding dong.

LAURIE *doesn't move to answer.*

(*Long and impatient.*) Ding dong ding dong ding dong ding dong.

LAURIE *goes to imaginary door and opens it.* MRS PROCTOR *walks through frame. She is wearing a trilby hat, man's coat, plastic bags over her shoes and carrying an umbrella.*

You took your time! I thought you were going to leave me standing on the doorstep all night. Aren't you going to give your mother a kiss? (*Embrace; over shoulder sees flat.*) What an untidy flat. You might have cleaned it up a bit for me.

LAURIE: Well, I wasn't expecting you to drip in on me like this, was I?

MRS PROCTOR (*shaking umbrella*): I've only popped round for a chat, Laurie. Now, would you be a dear and bring your mother's suitcases in? They're wet. If they get wet, Laurie, they'll be ruined.

LAURIE (*drags suitcases in during dialogue;* MRS PROCTOR *watches fondly*): Mother!

MRS PROCTOR: Aren't they beautiful? They were a Christmas present from David. We had a lovely Christmas together. What did you give me, Laurie? (*Takes off plastics.*)

LAURIE (*dumps first case in*): Nothing!

MRS PROCTOR: Just like your father.

LAURIE (*dragging in second case*): That's not surprising, he's been dead for years.

MRS PROCTOR: Aye, and it won't be long before I join him.

LAURIE: I hope you haven't come to spend your last days with me. That's to be David's privilege, remember? (*Slams door.*) SLAM!

MRS PROCTOR: Things are a little bit difficult between your brother and myself at the moment.

LAURIE: Oh dear, what now. Has he been feeding you scraps again?

MRS PROCTOR: I know I'm a terrible burden, I'm the first to admit it . . .

LAURIE: How can you say you're a terrible burden. You've got your own room . . .

MRS PROCTOR: I'd like to see you sleeping in the dog house.

LAURIE: With air-conditioning, which cost him a lot of money to put in.

MRS PROCTOR: Money! There you are, you see, money, NOT love.

LAURIE: Lots of mothers would love to have what you have.

MRS PROCTOR (*taking off hat, thinks*):

. . . Erica Jong's mother's got a fur coat. (*Puts hat on dummy.*)

LAURIE: Erica Jong's got a zipless purse, I haven't. You'll have to ask David for that sort of thing.

MRS PROCTOR: Ask David? Haven't you been listening to a word I've said? Did you know your brother's threatened to put me away?

LAURIE (*removing* MRS PROCTOR's *wet articles, gloves etc. from where she's put them*): . . . Well it's hardly the first time, is it?

MRS PROCTOR: You don't know how hurtful he's been to me, ME his own flesh and blood.

LAURIE: Should do, I've heard about it often enough. You know perfectly well he's tearing down the motorway right now, give him two hours and he'll be your precious David again. So don't get settled, put your plastics back on, you're coming with me. I've got to go over to Covent Garden with these designs.

MRS PROCTOR: Laurie! It's nearly ten o'clock. I've only just got here. You cannot rush around at my age. Surely your mother's more important than some grotty little stall in Covent Garden.

LAURIE: Some grotty little stall in Covent Garden?

MRS PROCTOR: That little junk stall you've got, though how you can make a living at that beats me.

LAURIE: When was the last time you went to Covent Garden?

MRS PROCTOR: What you do in public is your own business.

LAURIE: Exactly, because if you had any interest in me at all, you would know that I now own a dress shop in Covent Garden. An extremely successful dress shop. I could become a chain if I wanted to.

MRS PROCTOR: It's a step up the ladder, I suppose.

LAURIE: It's not a ladder, it's a sheer cliff, and I'm scared of heights.

MRS PROCTOR: Have you no one to help you, give you advice?

LAURIE: I don't need any help.

MRS PROCTOR: What about your flatmate? (*Sniffs around in the air.*) Or haven't you got one?

LAURIE (*over-defensively*): Of course I've got one. Whatever makes you think I haven't?

MRS PROCTOR: Mother's instinct.

LAURIE (*stammer*): He's just not very interested in the business world, that's all.

MRS PROCTOR: So you're all on your own.

LAURIE: I can cope perfectly well on my own.

MRS PROCTOR: It's getting you down though, isn't it? I can tell. You NEED someone to look after you. (*Reaches out to embrace LAURIE who runs across the room towards the dummy.*)

LAURIE: I'm fine. Don't worry about me.

MRS PROCTOR: I DO worry about you, I can't help but worry, you're my only daughter.

LAURIE: You only worry about me when it suits you.

MRS PROCTOR: I worry about the emptiness of your life.

LAURIE: Worry about your own.

MRS PROCTOR: I do.

LAURIE: Well, why don't you stop worrying and do something about it?

MRS PROCTOR: David could make me feel useful only he never lets me do anything for him.

LAURIE: Oh come off it, Mum, David's very good to you.

MRS PROCTOR: He doesn't need me anymore.

LAURIE: It's the old Oedipus complex; they all go through it.

MRS PROCTOR: I've done something terrible, Laurie, and this is my punishment.

LAURIE: Oh mother, you're always being thrown out of Paradise. It's the way you dress, it's most disconcerting.

MRS PROCTOR: This time it's a little higher up the list than 'Thou shalt not covet men's clothing'.

LAURIE: I don't care. You're NOT staying here. I've got a lot on my

dummies at the moment, and (*Emphatic.*) my flatmate wouldn't like it, he needs peace and quiet in the day time. (*Inspiration.*) ... He's a writer.

MRS PROCTOR: Oh, oh, it's a long time since I've been with a man with letters. Oh, not since I developed a taste for dangerous sex. Is he here?

LAURIE: No, he's gone out.

MRS PROCTOR: I'd like to see his room. He won't mind obliging a lady, it's not too much to ask.

LAURIE: No. Mother! (*Stops her physically.*)

MRS PROCTOR: You're ashamed of me, that's what it boils down to. You think I should be put away too, don't you?

LAURIE: Oh Mum!

MRS PROCTOR: Don't Oh Mum me! You probably won't put my name on the headstone.

LAURIE: Probably not. We're having you cremated and your ashes thrown to the wind ... it's cheaper.

MRS PROCTOR (*clasping heart on wrong side*): Laurie. How could you say such a thing? How could you be so CRUEL to your own mother?

LAURIE: Easily, and your heart's on the other side. It's not the sort of organ they can swap around.

MRS PROCTOR: My God, you'll regret that when I'm gone.

LAURIE: Tell me where you're going and I'll drive you there.

MRS PROCTOR: I'm going OUT ... I can't expect to be fed here.

LAURIE (*not flinching*): You're quite right. There's nothing in the fridge but a bad smell. Save your tantrums for David, men are much more appreciative.

MRS PROCTOR: I can see there's no point in talking to you now, but when the time comes you'll do your duty by me. You're my daughter don't forget. (*Exits without hat and slams door.*) SLAM!

LAURIE: Duty ... what a horrible four-letter word.

She returns to dummy. JOANNA arrives, plays doorbell dejectedly.

JOANNA: Ding dong.

LAURIE *considers not opening. Doorbell rings again.*

Ding dong.

LAURIE *picks up mother's hat off dummy. Goes to open door, expecting it to be her mother, extends hat without looking toward the door.*

LAURIE: Forgotten something? Oh . . . hello (*Warm, excited.*) . . . I thought you were my mother. Come on in. It's been ages since I've seen you. (*Kiss.*) I'd given you up for dead.

JOANNA (*enters with suitcase of mother's belongings*): I think I'm going to be sick. (*Pukes into* MRS PROCTOR's *hat.*)

LAURIE: Are you in love?

JOANNA: No.

LAURIE: Good, that means we can have an adult conversation. Cup of tea, coffee, chocolate, brandy?

JOANNA: Brandy.

LAURIE: Actually I haven't got any.

JOANNA *cries.*

Oh Jo, don't cry, please. I hate disappointing people . . . I'll get some tomorrow.

JOANNA: I've just been mugged.

LAURIE: Oh no, how shocking.

JOANNA: Two of them. They snatched my portfolio. I've lost everything – documents, papers . . . If they fall into the wrong hands they could do irrevocable damage.

LAURIE: It's not so terrible. You'll have to start a new life with a new cheque card and the fear of someone else donating your kidneys, but I'll help you. Tell me all about it.

JOANNA: I was on my way to the Gents at Charing Cross . . .

LAURIE: Hoping to meet a shady character for your new book.

JOANNA: No. I was hoping to find my father actually.

LAURIE: I know it well. My father used to take me there and beg my mother to come home.

JOANNA: Did you ever see a man with a red face?

LAURIE: Several. My mother was a constant source of embarrassment.

JOANNA (*disappointed, then ironic*): I suppose you find it odd that I should want to know who my father was?

LAURIE: Only because there are so few men worth knowing.

JOANNA: It's suddenly become very important to me.

LAURIE: Did Marilyn put you up to this? She seems to think you're too dependent on your mother.

JOANNA: I am . . . I was . . . once very close.

LAURIE: WAS. That's it, you see. Start searching for your father and your mother goes to hang. (JOANNE *grabs her own throat.*) Aaah! Not that there's any love lost between me and mine. (*Pause.*) Really I should be the lesbian, not you.

JOANNA: Why shouldn't I be? I'm a woman. I've a right to be a lesbian like everybody else. Try it if you think it's so easy. I'd have thought you'd have tried everything.

LAURIE: You'd think so, wouldn't you? I mix with enough women. But no, I'm still a Harvey Wallbanger. It's the only way I can do it. Lying down seems like such a commitment. I think I could do it with a woman, but I'm not sure there'd be much difference. Take you and Marilyn, for instance.

JOANNA: For WHAT instance? How would you know what the difference is?

LAURIE: Well, I can only speak for myself, but . . .

JOANNA: That's all you can do, speak and talk for yourself. I have been traumatised today more times than I care to relate, and all you can do is criticise my sexuality . . . and I thought you were attracted to me. (*About to leave.*)

LAURIE: Hang on, Joanna. I didn't ask you to come here and seduce me, nor did I ask you to throw up in my mother's hat, but I do expect to be able to make an awkward pass at somebody in my own home.

A sickening thud. (*Bangs Harvey the dummy on head.*)
A struggle, a fight. A cruel night,
a cruel night.

JOANNA *makes struggling noises.*

And then the gags and gurgles
Of sweet life squeezed

JOANNA *gags and gurgles.*

Unmercifully like a blackhead.
Till all breath ceased.

JOANNA *and* MRS PROCTOR *attack the dummy.* LAURIE *enters with bottle of whisky and switches on the light.*

LAURIE: *Click* . . . Mother, what the hell do you think you're doing.

MRS PROCTOR (*on floor strangling Harvey the dummy,* JOANNA *is kneeling beside her*): We're only playing, Laurie.

LAURIE: Not with Harvey, you're not.

JOANNA: My mother and I used to do it – it's fun.

LAURIE: Look at his suit. And where's his *head*.

MRS PROCTOR: Poor Harvey. Never mind, we'll take him to the dolly hospital.

LAURIE: That's *it*. I'm calling David. (*On phone.*) Hello . . . his sister . . . No, I'm *not* a nurse! Just you tell him, whoever you are, that his mother's arriving on the first train tomorrow morning with my regards. (*Slam.*) He can't be disturbed, my arse!

MRS PROCTOR: I told you he didn't want me back.

LAURIE: He hasn't got a choice in the matter.

MRS PROCTOR: Well, if he's not coming for me I think I might go and see a few pals of mine; I feel quite randy after that little romp with Harvey.

LAURIE: You're *not* going anywhere. I want you in bed! I *want* everybody in bed.

MRS PROCTOR: But it's far too early, I like to go out at this time . . .

LAURIE: Go out if you like, but you won't get back in again.

MRS PROCTOR: Then where will I sleep? Not in here. I don't think I can with all these dummies staring at me. (*Points to the audience.*) It's like Madame 'Two Sods'.

LAURIE: All right. You can have the spare room . . . I mean Joanna's room.

MRS PROCTOR: Oh how lovely. I'm sure I shall be very comfortable in the spare room. Well, don't you two young ones stay up much longer. It's been a long and tiring day for some of us. Good night, love, night Joanna. Good night, Harvey, don't forget to take your slippers off before you go to bed.

She picks up cases, looking for help, gets none. Exits towards bedroom, grunting.

LAURIE: Joanna, honestly what *did* you think you were doing? . . .

JOANNA *has been sitting getting slowly sloshed.*

It's one thing to play along as my flatmate, it's another thing entirely to encourage one's mother to go around attacking male models, just when I thought she'd lost interest in that sort of thing.

JOANNA (*plays with* LAURIE*'s hair*): The beast in the belly manifests itself in all sorts of ways.

LAURIE: And I turned to lesbians to find normality.

JOANNA: I don't mind sleeping with you tonight. It would be good for my identity. But I can't make any promises.

LAURIE (*takes away bottle*): Are you willing? (*Taking off* JOANNA*'s shoes.*)

JOANNA: Will doesn't come into it. My body is beyond my control.

LAURIE: Already? Never mind, I've learned how to stagger it.

JOANNA: But I must tell you I won't be able to make love on kitchen cupboards massaging in coconut oil in time to Joan Armatrading. My mind's otherwise engaged.

LAURIE: Then you must free your mind. Listen to your body . . . the ebbs and flows of physical desire. (*Touches* JOANNA.)

JOANNA: The pounding and crashing of waves on the ocean floor?

LAURIE: Use whatever metaphor you like, just *let go*.

JOANNA: I can't swim.

LAURIE: I'll be your waterwings.

JOANNA: I've never *used* sexual aids.

LAURIE: Joanna. We are two women, adult and sexually mature. We don't need help from anyone or anything.

JOANNA *consents.* LAURIE *takes her hand as they go to the bedroom.*

(*Just before exit:*) Let's take the whisky with us, shall we?

JOANNA *and* LAURIE *exit left. Music for* MRS PROCTOR's *entrance: 'It's Raining Men' by the Weather Girls.*
    MRS PROCTOR *enters, having waited for them to go to bed and has changed into her clubbing gear – Divine drag with moustache and leather cap, wig, high heels. She picks up her keys from the table.*

MRS PROCTOR: Sorry, Harvey, you've got to stay here. Pity. I'm sure you'd be a big hit with the boys. (*Exits to right, speaking to audience.*) Oh, I'd take a break for ten minutes if I were you because I'm going out. *Slam.*

Lights.

Scene Three
LAURIE's *flat, next morning 11.00 a.m.*

Set is arranged as night before. Birds sing and twitter, a cock crows offstage. LAURIE *enters left wearing pyjamas designed by herself. She carries a tray with coffee pot, two cups, vase with silk flowers. She is singing 'Oh what a beautiful morning'.* MRS PROCTOR *enters singing softly 'It's Raining Men'. She drunkenly tries to fit key into lock.*
    LAURIE *tidies up the flat, puts her mother's things, including the hat with vomit in it, back into the suitcase. She does not hear her mother come in.* MRS PROCTOR *sneaks in behind her back, dives behind the sofa, throws the keys up into the air and disappears off into her bedroom.* LAURIE *picks up the keys and looks viperishly towards her mother's bedroom.* JOANNA *enters from*

LAURIE's *bedroom wearing identical pyjamas and only one sock.*

LAURIE: Morning!

JOANNA: What time is it?

LAURIE: Eleven o'clock. Doesn't time fly when you're in love?

JOANNA: Damn. I've overslept. Is there any coffee?

LAURIE: I've just made a pot. *Your* cup's over there.

JOANNA: *My* cup?

LAURIE: Yes, as in my cup overfloweth at the joy of seeing you again.

JOANNA *smells the coffee; it has an odd smell, tastes worse.* LAURIE *sees her reaction.*

It's imitation. I couldn't bear the thought of all those exploited Bolivians and Kenyans. I was beginning to taste the sweat and blood of the plantations.

JOANNA: It's *fake*, like everything else around here.

LAURIE: Joanna, when will you believe me. I swear I was not pretending. For years I was an *aaaahhh* (*Sings a note.*) Now I find I'm an *aaaaahhhhh* (*Sings same note again but either higher or lower.*) I was discovering the full extent of my range, that's all. Surely you weren't keeping anything hidden from *me*?

JOANNA: Do you think the only skeleton a lesbian has in her closet is her sexuality?

LAURIE: There's more to that sentence than meets the eye, and you're *not* meeting my eye, Joanna.

JOANNA: I suffer from life vertigo. If I looked anywhere but straight ahead I'd fall over.

LAURIE: If you do I'll be there to catch you. I'll be your safety net.

JOANNA: I couldn't ask you to be that. I'm weak. You'd have to be with me day and night, your whole life would revolve around mine, your shoulders would sag with my responsibilities, my failures would be yours, it would be wonderful . . . contrary to lesbian ethics.

LAURIE: I'm tired of being ethical. In a

few years I'll be old enough to be a 'role model'. I'd like to experience self-sacrifice before then.

JOANNA: Don't rush me, I need time to think it over. I wouldn't want to fall prey to gratitude.

LAURIE: Your very existence would be my thanks.

JOANNA: I suspect I might take advantage of you. I am utterly selfish. I even want to keep my sex to myself.

LAURIE: Its secludity is assured. Your genitals shall never leave my hands.

JOANNA: What about your mother? I insist there be no other woman in your life.

LAURIE: A night without sheets and blankets will have cooled her maternal passion.

JOANNA: Her name must never come between us. My problems must consume you utterly. Oh Laurie, I could not even bear it if you were breastfed.

LAURIE: I swear I have known only your mammary glands. Trust me.

JOANNA: I shall have such a lot to share with you. To *share*, Laurie, because with a woman nobody serves anybody and nobody expects to be served.

MRS PROCTOR (*booms offstage*): Laurie, where's *my* breakfast. (*Enters.*) You know I always have breakfast at this time in the morning.

MRS PROCTOR *has had a night on the tiles and enjoyed it. She is wearing a Janet Reger-type dressing gown, and swishes round the room smoking a cigarillo.*

David knows exactly what I want for breakfast; he brings it to me on a tray, and sometimes there's a red carnation in a silver bottle . . . Good morning, Joanna. I hope you're feeling better. Did you sleep well?

JOANNA: Yes, thank you.

MRS PROCTOR: Really? Didn't you find it a bit stuffy with all those sheets and blankets on top of you.

JOANNA: Oh, I *am* sorry. I forgot to mention I'd taken mine to the dry cleaners.

MRS PROCTOR: No need to be sorry, I brought my own. Morning Laurie, is there any chance of at least a cup of coffee for your mother?

LAURIE: You'll find everything you need in the kitchen.

MRS PROCTOR: My hands are a bit shaky in the morning, would you make it for me, there's a pal?

LAURIE, *not knowing whether this constitutes betrayal, looks at* JOANNA.

JOANNA: Yes please.

LAURIE *picks up pot.*

MRS PROCTOR: Oh, and while you're there, if you could fry an egg, I'll have it sunny side up.

LAURIE: There's no time for breakfast.

MRS PROCTOR: What's your hurry? We've missed at least four trains.

LAURIE: I want to make sure you don't miss the next one.

MRS PROCTOR: Oh well, I shall just have to go out to eat.

LAURIE: No. I'm not having you disappear for a whole day. You're staying put.

MRS PROCTOR: I've got to eat, Laurie, I'm wasting away.

LAURIE: All right, I'll go out and get something for all of us.

MRS PROCTOR: Sausage, bacon, eggs, chips will do me fine.

LAURIE *gets her shopping bag and purse.*

You're *not* going out dressed like that, are you?

LAURIE: Yes. Any objections?

MRS PROCTOR: No. If you want to get your slippers wet that's your business.

LAURIE *exits.*

Oohh! She is so bad-tempered in the morning.

JOANNA: I'm rather that way myself.

MRS PROCTOR: Not me. I'm always glad to get up and face a new day. (*Pause.*) I'm sure it's not very good for Laurie to see your long face over the breakfast table.

JOANNA: I beg your pardon?

MRS PROCTOR: Don't beg, sell matches. It's time we had a little chat, Joanna. Now don't get me wrong, it's nothing personal, but I'm worried about my daughter, as any mother would be. I think it's very unhealthy the way she's living. Keeping odd hours, eating odd meals, associating with *odd* people, and what's worse, if she doesn't watch out, she'll be a nymphomaniac before she knows it. She already can't tell one Harvey from another . . . I've read all about it in *Woman's Own*. If you substitute Harvey for Willy you'll know what I mean . . . Maybe you wouldn't, you're not old enough to read *Woman's Own*.

JOANNA: Don't you think Laurie's old enough to know what she's doing?

MRS PROCTOR: That's just it, I don't think she does, and although I hesitate to say it, I don't think you're helping her with your flighty ways.

JOANNA: I shall never take flight from Laurie.

MRS PROCTOR: My daughter may have her faults, but she is *not* an airport. If I say you're bad for her, you're *bad* for her, and I don't want anything bad to happen to my Laurie.

JOANNA: Neither would I, Mrs Proctor, I assure you. Your daughter has been more than good to me.

MRS PROCTOR: You only get the scraps of her affection. My daughter would do more for me than for anybody else in the whole wide world, and when the time comes when she'll have to choose between us I know who she'll put first.

JOANNA: And what if she doesn't put you first?

MRS PROCTOR: Oh you mean if she's confused? Well I'd have to make it easier for her. I'm a wee bit psychic, Joanna . . . get it from my grandmother, Scots maternal . . . and I'm getting this dreadful feeling that you might meet with a terrible accident, an accident that could well be fatal. If my grandmother's name's not *Gambell*.

JOANNA: *Gambell*?

MRS PROCTOR: Aye, Gambell of the Black Gambells.

Doorbell rings. MRS GAMBELL is out of vision of front door. JOANNA opens door.

1ST MUGGER (*walks in boldly followed by* SECOND MUGGER): Hello, remember us?

JOANNA: Yes, you're the two that mugged me last night.

MRS PROCTOR *grasps chain round neck and dives behind the sofa.*

2ND MUGGER (*upper-class accent*): We've got a little something for you. (*Shyly hands over a nicely wrapped parcel.*)

JOANNA (*rips it open*): It's my portfolio, oh thank you.

2ND MUGGER: Don't thank me, thank Trev.

Big bashful smile from Walt Disney MUGGERS.

JOANNA: It's empty.

2ND MUGGER: Yes, well, you had some very valuable property in there, some very valuable property.

1ST MUGGER: We put it in a safe place. (*shows ticket from locker storage.*)

2ND MUGGER: In case we got mugged.

JOANNA: All right. How much do you want?

1ST MUGGER: Oh, we don't want money.

JOANNA (*addressing God*): Oh God, they want my kidneys.

2ND MUGGER: No, no, we want your brain. We want to be stars of your next paperback nasty.

JOANNA: Impossible. I take a pride in my work. You're just two ordinary muggers. I can't write a book about two ordinary muggers.

1ST MUGGER (*hurt*): Ordinary?

JOANNA: Let me put it in words of less than three syllables. Who have you mugged this week?

1ST MUGGER: Nobody really.

JOANNA: What about you? Were you ever on the police payroll, for example.

2ND MUGGER: Did a video once. Didn't get paid for it.

JOANNA: Precisely. Ordinary. If you can come up with something exciting then maybe I'll consider it, but I think we should settle this in the usual way, eh boys? Ten pounds enough?

She goes for purse in bag on sofa.
SECOND MUGGER *goes to accept.*

1ST MUGGER: What about the sudden disappearance of a thriller author, to be held hostage in her mum's cellar for months on end?

JOANNA: Now that . . .

2ND MUGGER: Right.

He grabs JOANNA *and puts hand over her mouth.* FIRST MUGGER *puts chlorine handkerchief over* JOANNA*'s mouth.* THE TWO MUGGERS *carry* JOANNA *out.*

1ST MUGGER: No point in struggling, miss, he's queer. Ha, Ha, Ha.

Exit.

MRS PROCTOR (*emerging from hiding place behind sofa*): I've said it before and I'll say it again, London is a very dangerous city. Not even your own victim is safe in your hands. *Slam!* *Ring ring, ring ring, ring ring.* Hello . . . Hello David . . . No, she's out . . . Yes, I've explained the situation . . . I think she realises that . . . No, you won't have to, she's going to take me in. Mm, Mm, Mm David . . . Would you lend me money for an operation? . . . David! (*Puts phone down.*)

Enter LAURIE.

LAURIE: I don't know why they bothered with those lifts, they're always getting stuck. (*Seeing nothing has changed.*) Mum, you might have at least set the table, and why haven't you got dressed? There's your breakfast. (*Chucks a paper bag on the sofa.*)

MRS PROCTOR: But this is yoghurt and I ordered bacon and eggs.

LAURIE: Yoghurt's better for you, and no one has to cook and wash up afterwards.

MRS PROCTOR: Can't I at least have toast? What's in there?

LAURIE: That's Jo's and my lunch. Never mind, you can always have a sandwich on the train. Jo in the bathroom?

MRS PROCTOR: Oh her? She's gone. Just went, without a by your leave.

LAURIE: Did you say something to upset her?

MRS PROCTOR: No more than the usual pleasantries.

LAURIE: Didn't she leave a note?

MRS PROCTOR: Do we have to report to you if we want to go anywhere?

LAURIE: Joanna is a free agent, we put no restrictions on each other whatsoever. Luckily it can keep for this evening.

MRS PROCTOR: I don't think she'll be back that soon. Never mind, I like a nice avocado.

LAURIE: What makes you think you're going to be here for dinner tonight?

MRS PROCTOR: Of course, you don't know, do you? David rang while you were out. He wanted to remind you that you had a mother too.

LAURIE (*taking things out of her shopping bag – real coffee, etc*): Who needs reminding?

MRS PROCTOR: He said that you were in a position now to be able to accept that responsibility.

LAURIE: I'm responsible for having you as a mother, don't make me laugh.

MRS PROCTOR: I told him not to worry. That you had taken me in and would look after me. I won't be much trouble, and I'll have the place prettied-up in no time, and we'll be as close as we were when you were just a tiny thing in my arms.

LAURIE: And where does Joanna fit into this?

MRS PROCTOR: We won't need anybody else, it'll be just you and me. Well, you can have one or two of your wee friends round, when I'm out.

LAURIE: Joanna, is more than just a wee friend. In fact we plan to be together rather a lot.

MRS PROCTOR: Laurie, I know something about Joanna that you don't. Believe me, she won't be back in a hurry.

LAURIE: Oh? Do you have carnal knowledge of Joanna too? Do you sleep in the same bed? Do you share your frilly nighties? Do you plan to have what one might call a marital relationship?

MRS PROCTOR: Carnal knowledge? Are you trying to tell me you lust after your own sex.

LAURIE: Is that so very strange to you?

MRS PROCTOR: No matter what I've been in the past, I've always been one thing, and that's consistent. But a *woman*? What do you do? Do you play with each other's breasts?

LAURIE: We don't play with each other's breasts, we make love.

MRS PROCTOR (*thinks; pause*): . . . Well, it won't last. I've read about these things, there's no bond between you, nothing to keep you together. I'm your mother, Laurie, and mothers are tied to their children. Ask any mother and she'll say the same. It's the one thing a woman can be certain about. So let's forget Joanna and imagine how happy we're going to be together.

LAURIE: It's like talking to a brick wall. What do you think you're doing? Go and get dressed, you've got a train to catch.

MRS PROCTOR (*innocent*): Who? Me? I'm not going anywhere.

LAURIE: Mother . . . Right, I'm calling the police. I am not above having you bodily thrown out.

MRS PROCTOR: No, Laurie. Not the police. I might confess. There's something about their uniform that inspires confidence. I can just see myself swooning on a blue serge suit, saying, 'It was me officer, I arranged to have my son's fiancée killed'. Just to be near its roughness.

LAURIE: You don't have to confess to murder if you want to be roughed around. Go on a march instead, you'll use up just as many calories.

MRS PROCTOR: But I have to confess to someone, Laurie, or I'll go mad. (*Shows* LAURIE *the chain round her neck with a gold finger on it.*) What do you think this is?

LAURIE: It's the second finger of a left hand rolled in gold . . . a woman's finger.

MRS PROCTOR: What woman that you and I know wears purple and yellow nail varnish?

LAURIE: I'm sure David's fiancée won't be the only one.

MRS PROCTOR: Bite the nail. What does it taste of?

LAURIE: Meths . . . It could be the preservative.

MRS PROCTOR: David's fiancée soaked her nails in meths to prevent her from biting them. That and the smell of sex was a lethal combination.

LAURIE: This nail is over an inch long, and shows no sign of being bitten. Good bluff, mother. (*Gives it back to her.*)

MRS PROCTOR: This nail has been dead a month. The finger touched God's six months ago.

LAURIE: What happened to the rest of her?

MRS PROCTOR: Decently buried. I had to have her killed, Laurie, she was coming between me and my only claim to a penis. (*Points to the phone.*) . . . Now do you want to call the police?

LAURIE: I don't think the police are equipped to deal with penis envy. Who else knows about this?

MRS PROCTOR: Nobody except you. David suspects I was behind it. He's offered to pay for a lobotomy. He said it would be cheaper than a rest home. It's not the sort of operation I had in mind, I can tell you. I don't want to end up in a home. You won't put me away, will you?

LAURIE: It won't come to that. No rest home would have you. David and I will have to work something out, and quickly. I don't know how we're going to do it, but we will. Now, we're both to remain sane and sensible about this, neither of us can think clearly in our nightwear, so we're going to get dressed and I'll drive you back to David's.

MRS PROCTOR: No. I'd rather kill myself first.

LAURIE: You'll do what I say, Mum, you can kill yourself afterwards. Go on.

MRS PROCTOR *exits to the bedroom. LAURIE thinks for a moment then goes to her bedroom to get changed. MRS PROCTOR shoots back onstage, picks up JOANNA's tie and charges out.*

MRS PROCTOR: Slam!

LAURIE *hears the door bang and runs out of her bedroom half-dressed.*

LAURIE: Mother!

Enter JOANNA on stage, covering mouth with a cloth. She is high on bleach.

JOANNA (*mesmerised*): Ding dong.

LAURIE (*rushes to answer*): Did you see my mother?

JOANNA: No, darling. I've been stuck in a lift with two claustrophobic kidnappers, a hanky and a bottle of bleach. If your mother had been there we'd have noticed her.

LAURIE: Do you want to invite your friends in? I'd like you to feel this place is your home.

JOANNA: They're no friends of mine. They're the two that mugged me last night. They must have followed me here.

LAURIE: What more could they want from you, sweetheart?

JOANNA: What everybody wants from me. Immortality.

LAURIE (*getting dressed*): Really.

JOANNA (*sniffing bleached hanky*): I tell you, Laurie. I have had revelations of Wildean proportion in that carpeted cell. What you see before you is not the starry-eyed lover of last night's embrace, nor the lilac-covered altar you offered yourself to this morning, but the face of a woman whose life has suddenly become fraught with danger, terror and dreadful hope.

LAURIE: It's a lovely face.

JOANNA: There are two men out there who fainted because a lift was too small for them.

LAURIE (*still getting dressed*): Oh yes.

JOANNA: The world is too small for me and every inch there is to be gained must be fought for, by me, on my own . . . This ticket will be my trial. It's a ticket to a locker in Charing Cross Station.

LAURIE: It doesn't alter my commitment to you one iota.

JOANNA: Oh yes. Could you still love me . . . knowing that I am the seed of a harvest of whom Death is the reaper?

LAURIE: Jo, stop talking in riddles. Tell me what is concealed in that locker. If it's the second finger of a left hand rolled in gold, I've seen it all before.

JOANNA: Where have you see it all before?

LAURIE: On a chain around my mother's neck. Death runs in more than one family, you know.

JOANNA: Does your mother have a bank account in Milton Keynes?

LAURIE: Yes, she calls it her operation account.

JOANNA: Where is she now?

LAURIE: She confessed to a hideous crime and ran off. I suspect she may commit suicide.

JOANNA: I must stop her. Now think, where would she have run to?

LAURIE: Well, when she threatened before, it was when she desperately needed a sex change.

JOANNA: I'll ring round all the hospitals.

LAURIE: No. She'll have gone to the Gents at Charing Cross for consolation. My mother is absolutely in love with men. It was so much simpler for her when she had a penis.

PRISON OFFICER *plays doorbell gloomily.*

PRISON OFFICER: Ding dong, dear.

LAURIE *opens, expecting to see her mother, and is shocked.*

HM Prisons. Good morning.

LAURIE: Oh, hello, Officer.

PRISON OFFICER: There's no need to be alarmed, Miss. It does my protection mania no good. My superior thinks I have an unhealthy interest in the weak and defenceless, yet they have been some of my greatest passions. Albeit short-lived.

LAURIE: My mother's not in. I haven't seen her for weeks.

JOANNA: It's all right, Laurie, I know this woman. Would you mind leaving us alone for a second.

LAURIE *looks* PRISON OFFICER *up and down, then looks at* JOANNA *and exits left.*

Please come in.

PRISON OFFICER: I count myself lucky to have found you, Madam. Had I not seen a rather oddly dressed person come out from this building, in possession of a tie I recognised to be yours, I would have been chasing a wild goose all day.

JOANNA: You've been to see my mother's lawyer?

PRISON OFFICER: No Madam, her mortician. Your Holy Mother's body has disappeared. Talk about rolling away the stone. What a woman. The management of course cannot be held responsible. You understand their position, a public menace still at large, very sticky . . . You having signed for her personal effects, which in our books includes her body, are obliged to undertake her retrieval. I feel I should offer my assistance.

JOANNA: Thank you, Prison Officer, but my mother has always considered herself solely responsible for her own body. She wouldn't ask anyone to do to her what she wouldn't do herself. I'm sure she'll not shirk her own burial.

PRISON OFFICER: I'm relieved to hear it, Madam. There are some acts which even I am not prepared to perform with a woman. Digging their grave is one of them.

JOANNA: My mother would not have loved you the less for it.

PRISON OFFICER: Well, if everything is under control I'd better be going,

otherwise 'that young friend' of yours might be jealous. I'm a handsome woman, I know.

JOANNA: Thank you again, Officer. We're both very touched by your concern.

PRISON OFFICER: Pleasure, Madam, and if anything takes you to Death Row again, do pop in and see me. Your mother was more than just a 'body' to me.

Exits.

LAURIE (*reappears*): Jo, what did she want? I heard mention of a body. What *have* you got concealed in that locker? Is there someone else in your life? Someone I mustn't know about?

JOANNA *presses locker ticket into* LAURIE'*s hand.*

Jo, where are you going?

JOANNA: To the Gents at Charing Cross. For it was there that the seed of discontent was sown.

Exits.

LAURIE: Jo!

LAURIE *is left with ticket to locker and decides to go and find out what's in it. Lights.*

Scene Four

Gents at Charing Cross.

The cast as 'Dirty Old Men' change the scene to the music 'My Heart Belongs to Daddy' sung by Eartha Kitt. MRS PROCTOR *uprights the sofa which spreads out as a urinal and carries the lavatory pedestal to the centre of the stage.* JOANNA, PRISON OFFICER *and* LAURIE *play men masturbating themselves and each other at the urinal while* MRS PROCTOR *steps onto a step-ladder beside the lavatory pedestal and tries to hang herself with* JOANNA'*s tie.*

MRS PROCTOR: Goodbye, cruel world. Goodbye.

No response from masturbators so she moves the ladder to the other side of the pedestal.

Goodbye, cruel world. Goodbye. (*About to jump.*) Oh, goodbye, cruel world. *Goodbye.*

MONA *enters in ghostly prison clothes, ribbon of Scene One round her neck, looking like death warmed up. Drags herself like a tired Zombie; she's searching for* JOANNA *and walks past* MRS PROCTOR.

Stand back. Don't move – I want to kill myself. (*No response from* MONA.) Excuse *me*, this is a Gents' toilet. Men only.

MONA: I'm disembodied. I'm not subject to any access code.

She approaches MRS PROCTOR.

MRS PROCTOR: Leave me alone. I want to end it all.

MONA: That noose isn't strong enough to hang a feather duster.

MRS PROCTOR: You're somebody's wife, aren't you? You'd be happy to see me die.

MONA: I never married, it seemed like a cold-blooded thing to do. Are you a regular here?

MRS PROCTOR: Nobody here is regular. We pride ourselves upon it.

MONA: I'm looking for my daughter, perhaps you know of her?

MRS PROCTOR: What does she call herself?

MONA: Joanna.

MRS PROCTOR: I know a Henrietta, a Gertrude and an Olivia, but I've never come across a Joanna . . . Joanna lacks sexual drive.

MONA: So she tells me.

MRS PROCTOR: Joanna, Henrietta, Gertrude and Olivia, this is for you.

MONA: Have you got a daughter?

MRS PROCTOR: Yes. No, I've turned my back on her.

MONA: Will she be terribly upset when she hears you're dead?

MRS PROCTOR: Everyone will be better off when I'm gone.

MONA: Would you mind stepping down for a minute? I have rather a stiff neck.

MRS PROCTOR: Are you trying to save my life?

MONA: Save it? I'm on borrowed time myself.

MRS PROCTOR: All right. I'll come down and unburden myself to you. (*Holds chain around neck.*)

MONA: You're not going to pull any crucifixes on me, are you?

MRS PROCTOR: At my age all I can pull is a muscle, especially after a night on the tiles. (*Points around her and laughs.*) Ha, ha, ha, 'a night on the tiles' . . . You're looking a bit on the peaky side yourself.

MONA: I am plagued with doubt, everywhere I see treachery and defeat. This has had an adverse effect on my complexion.

MRS PROCTOR: You've kept your figure at least. You'll have no trouble attracting men.

MONA: I'm not interested in men. There have been more important things in my life.

MRS PROCTOR: Motherhood? Give me a man anytime. Manipulating the male sex has been one of the most satisfying experiences of my life. Some nights the toilets are full of the charming young things. And on those nights I feel I must be very close to Heaven.

MONA: I was a single mother. I put the whole of my *being* into my child. Sex never reared her ugly head.

MRS PROCTOR: It didn't harm mine. Both of my children turned out attractive.

MONA: Had I been a more conventional mother, instilled feelings of duty, loyalty and sacrifice in her, she might not have failed me so.

MRS PROCTOR: Duty, loyalty and sacrifice? They're not the sort of thing children understand.

MONA: I have lived a full life and all I have to show for it is a weak and thankless daughter who thinks nothing of abandoning me to search for her father. It was here that she was conceived twenty-five years ago. (*Pointing to toilet seat.*) and it is here that she thinks she will find her (*– spoken as a nasty word.*) *identity.*

MRS PROCTOR: Have you no sins you could visit upon her, if she's in doubt, so she could have some idea of where she's coming from?

MONA: Nothing that I consider a sin.

MRS PROCTOR: Conception out of wedlock must count as one.

A look from MONA.

(*Hurriedly.*) . . . Among Christian folk.

MONA: I suspect her father was married, but took to sowing his seed on barren ground.

MRS PROCTOR: I've always wanted to father a child. All those bits of me going to waste, I used to think. But twenty-five years ago, in that very toilet, I made the decision to return to womanhood, for the sake of my husband and my little girl. I should never have done it. Sex hasn't been the same since.
   I have written a poem to my children which I would like to have found about my body. (*Reads poem written on her arm, leg, etc.*)

I bore him a boy, David.	
The boy loved a girl.	Our manhood
I bore the girl evil.	My castration
The boy bore me no longer.	My freedom
I found others to bore me.	My punishment
I've left it unfinished – all the best composers do.	My cost

MONA: That tie! It's my daughter's.

MRS PROCTOR: No, it's my daughter's lesbian lover's. Its Joanna's.

MONA: Fool! Joanna is *my* daughter. (*Pulling* MRS PROCTOR *by her tie.*)

MRS PROCTOR: Who are you calling a fool?

MONA: Where is she?

MRS PROCTOR: She's been kidnapped.

MONA: Kidnapped? Then I've misjudged her badly.

MRS PROCTOR *gives her a look of 'oh no you haven't'.*

You say she has a lover? Is she happy with this woman?

MRS PROCTOR: Of course she is. My daughter's a lovely person.

MONA: How nearly I ruined it all.

MRS PROCTOR: You tried. Why don't we make this a double hanging. I'll let you have Jo's tie. (*Holds out her arm to* MONA.) Here, you can add a P.S. asking her for forgiveness.

Bell tolls.

MONA: It's too late. My time has finally come.

MRS PROCTOR: Rubbish. Everybody forgives the dead. I'm expecting a martyrhood myself.

Sound effects of ghosts.

MONA (*shaking her head*): They're coming for me.

MRS PROCTOR: They always find out where you are in the end. (*Tries to keep* MONA *with her.*)

MONA: Can you hear them calling my name? Mona! Mona!

MRS PROCTOR: At least they want you back.

MONA: I can't hold on much longer. Give this to my child. (*Ribbon around her neck from Scene One.*) and tell her I rest in peace.

Exits.

MRS PROCTOR: I *can't* hold on much longer. I can't hold on much longer . . . That voice – twenty-five years ago. I remember it as if it were yesterday. (*Looks towards toilet seat.*)

JOANNA (*turns round from urinal*): Stop. Don't do it. Please don't kill yourself.

MRS PROCTOR: Joanna, Joanna. Why, I couldn't do that. I have everything to live for now. Your darling mother has made me see my life for what it is.

JOANNA: Mother was here?

MRS PROCTOR: We met like ships in the night and then she passed on. She left you this ribbon, and she wants you to know she rests in peace.

JOANNA *looks at the ribbon.*

Is it perhaps the ribbon you wore in your hair as a child? You had unruly hair when you were little, didn't you? (*Ruffles* JOANNA's *hair.*)

JOANNA: She had it cut off.

MRS PROCTOR: And you had to wear braces on your front teeth, didn't you? So did I. You blush easily too. I can see that. You're your father's daughter all right.

JOANNA: You know my father.

MRS PROCTOR (nods): I only realised today how closely we're related. I am your missing link.

JOANNA: You?

MRS PROCTOR: That toilet seat will stand witness to my impregnation of your mother, twenty-five years ago.

JOANNA: I don't believe it!

MRS PROCTOR: A toilet seat would have no reason to lie.

JOANNA: You must have been a man then.

MRS PROCTOR: I'm glad your mother didn't skimp on the facts of life. I'm not sure I'd have been the right person to tell you.

JOANNA: Are you Laurie's father too?

MRS PROCTOR: No, no. I've always been Laurie's mother. It's an arrangement we have.

JOANNA: You've put me in a very awkward position, Mrs Proctor.

MRS PROCTOR: I know I haven't been very nice to you in the past. But I'll make it up to you, Joanna, I promise.

JOANNA: I wish you wouldn't keep saying my name as if it were a miracle.

MRS PROCTOR: Every child needs someone for whom she is a miracle. I wouldn't want you to be deprived of that. (Approaches to embrace.)

JOANNA (ribbon in hand as a reminder, turns away): What have you got around your neck, Mrs Gambell?

MRS PROCTOR: Your tie.

JOANNA: Not the second finger of a left hand rolled in gold.

MRS PROCTOR: Yes. You can have it if you like, as a christening present.

She takes it off. JOANNA turns round; it is almost handed over.

You called me Mrs Gambell, how did you come by that name?

JOANNA: My mother was paid by a Mrs Gambell of Milton Keynes, to squeeze the life out of a young woman.

MRS PROCTOR: The mother of my child is a professional assassin!

JOANNA: Was a professional assassin. My mother was hanged for the murder you committed. That was her corpse you talked to.

MRS PROCTOR: I thought she looked far from well.

JOANNA: Her last wish was that I track this Mrs Gambell to her lair, force her to reveal her identity, and expose her to the public.

MRS PROCTOR: How would I give myself away?

JOANNA: She told me you would be in possession of an unusual trinket, the second finger of a left hand – rolled in gold.

MRS PROCTOR: I knew it would be my downfall, but I'm a sentimental old fool. (Holds out her wrists as if to be handcuffed.) There, I deliver myself into your hands. Have mercy. Remember, for twenty-five years I bore you no ill. I'd like that taken into account.

JOANNA: You were responsible for the death of my mother, I can give you no credit for that.

MRS PROCTOR: I was responsible for your birth too. You couldn't have done it on your own.

No response from JOANNA to plea.

I am your father, for fuck's sake!

JOANNA: I must expose you, don't you understand, or I'll live in an identity crisis for the rest of my life.

MRS PROCTOR: Then I'll kill myself.

JOANNA: No, I need you.

MRS PROCTOR: I'll have that sex change. It's what I want. It's my life, your mother showed me that. (Flicking first right breast, then left.) You can have your Mrs Gambell, your Mrs Proctor. You can even have my daughter. You can have everything you want only leave *my* identity.

JOANNA: I could have everything I want, my way, without a fight. I could be a writer of fiction again. Mrs Gambell doesn't exist.

MRS PROCTOR: She won't – not in any form. The op. is a hundred per cent. You'll have a whole father.

JOANNA: What the hell, I'll do it.

MRS PROCTOR: I'll have to pawn this and I'll need some money for a down-payment.

JOANNA *gives her a wad of notes.* LAURIE *turns round from urinal.*

Laurie?

LAURIE: Mother. (*To* JOANNA.) I've brought you your papers.

JOANNA: Darling, that shows you validate my existence.

LAURIE: What I bring you is stronger than a locker, mightier than maternal love, and more powerful still than the stench of the sewers that draws you here.

MRS PROCTOR: Did you bring me anything to eat?

JOANNA: Laurie, this is my father.

MRS PROCTOR: Haven't I got a name?

JOANNA: Laurie, this is my father, Mrs Proctor.

LAURIE: Impossible.

MONA *enters. She sees money in* MRS PROCTOR's *hands.*

MONA: My maintenance!

JOANNA: Mummy!

MRS PROCTOR (*money taken out of her hands by* MONA): Dearest?

JOANNA (*to* LAURIE): Sister.

LAURIE: Lover!

MRS PROCTOR: Incest.

LAURIE (*to* MRS PROCTOR): Sisterhood!

PRISON OFFICER *turns round from urinal with keys in hand.*

PRISON OFFICER (*making a clicking noise as if unlocking a door*): Cosy!

Lights. Two freeze shots of Victorian family. Bow.

Blackout.

The Rug of Identity

This is my third play and I still don't have a toaster . . .

Jill Fleming
1987

List of plays performed by Hard Corps

1983/4   *For She's A Jolly Good Fellow* by Jill Fleming
A farce about political manipulation, artistic freedom, closet lesbians and small-town communities . . .

1983/4   *Lovers and Other Enemies* by Jill Fleming
The bizarre, passionate and hilarious attempts of the characters to find the answer to the eternal question 'which comes first – the sex or the politics?' The struggles of individuals who don't give a damn or have trouble understanding the question . . .

1984/5   *John* by Adèle Saleem
A theatrical account of the relationship between Marguerite Radclyffe Hall, author of *The Well of Loneliness*, and Una, Lady Troubridge.

1985   *Les Autres (That Lot)* by Sarah McNair
A play about Renée Vivien, Natalie Barney and Romaine Brooks – the lesbian community of Paris in the early part of this century.

1985   *For Ever* Hard Corps in association with Parker and Klein
A revue centred around a lesbian feminist orgy . . .

1986   *The Rug of Identity* by Jill Fleming